Reflective Language Teaching

Reflective Language Teaching

From Research to Practice

Thomas S. C. Farrell

continuum

Continuum

The Tower Building
11 York Road
London SE1 7NX

80 Maiden Lane, Suite 704
New York
NY 10038

© Thomas S. C. Farrell November 2007

British Library Cataloguing-in-Publication Data
A catalogue record for this book is available from the British Library.

ISBNS: 978–08264–9657–7 (hardback)
        978–08264–9658–4 (paperback)

Library of Congress Cataloging-in-Publication Data

A catalog record for this book is available from the library of congress.

Typeset by Aptara, Inc., New Delhi, India
Printed and bound in Great Britain by Athenaeum Press, Gateshead, Tyne & Wear

Contents

Preface

Reflective Language Teaching is a book unique in existence because it presents up-to-date research on reflective language teaching and also presents case studies, most of which have been conducted by this author in collaboration with other language teachers, that illustrate topics covered in each chapter. *Reflective Language Teaching* is for second language teachers interested in pursuing their own professional development. It can be used by individual teachers, pairs and groups of teachers informally or it can be used as a textbook for inservice language teacher development courses as well as for language teacher preparation courses. The book can also be used as a source book for school/institution heads and principals, directors and administrators who want to encourage their language teachers to think critically about their work. The real value of reflection is in separating thought and emotion from the teaching event. Once teachers come to understand the how and why of what they do and have done, they can then take steps that will carry them along the path to making more informed decisions in the classroom because now they have more choices. Beginning teachers too can find much in the contents of this book to orient them to the field of second language teaching. For example, the research that is presented can be read in its original form by locating original articles and also beginning teachers can begin reflecting on their practice by attempting to look at the various topics presented in the book either alone or with a critical friend.

Structure of the book

Each chapter in the book attempts to help teachers uncover aspects of their work that may otherwise remain at the tacit level. Chapter 1 gives a brief overview of reflective teaching and reflective language teaching. Chapters 2 to 13 demonstrate how teachers can reflect **ON** various aspects of their work and **WITH** various reflective tools: Chapters 2, 3, 4, 5, 6 and 7 (six chapters) outline how teachers can reflect *ON* the self, beliefs, narratives, language proficiency, metaphors and maxims, and classroom communication while Chapters 8, 9, 10, 11, 12 and 13 (six chapters) outline how teachers can reflect *WITH* action research, teaching journals, teacher development groups, classroom observations, critical friendships and concept maps. The final chapter (Chapter 14) attempts to bring it all together by providing a framework for reflective language teaching and also outlines a workshop on how teachers can generate topics for reflection.

Each chapter (except Chapter 1) is organized using a template that starts with an introduction to the chapter, and this is followed by *what the research says*, and *a case study* related to the topic of the chapter. The research section of each chapter attempts to highlight what has been researched most recently within language teaching only on the particular topic of that chapter. However, in case teachers are pressed for time (and really which teachers are not!), I have attempted to summarize the research in bullet form so you can just skim this section quickly and have a general overview of what has been done up to this point in time. Later if/when you have time, you can look in more depth at some of these studies and even read the actual papers/studies themselves as they are all in the references at the end of the book. In each case study, I attempt to outline an example of actual work I have carried out or directly participated in over the past 15 years because it has been suggested that while reflective teaching is attractive, not much actual research has been carried out as to its effectiveness. I hope these case studies will give further validity not only to the concept of reflective teaching but also to the contents of this book. Following the case study in each chapter, is the practical application of each activity, called *from research to practice*. This section of each chapter provides language teachers with many practical suggestions for implementing the particular topic or activity that was outlined in the early part of the chapter and is followed by a conclusion. Most of the practical suggestions are based on this author's personal experience working in this research area for the past 15 years but creative teachers will also come up with their own suggestions and/or adapt the suggestions provided in each chapter to their own contexts and needs. Each chapter also has a number of reflective questions which are placed after each case study, and at the end of each chapter. Also different scenarios are at the end of each chapter that reflect real-life happenings of language teachers and are a composite of this author's experiences in language teacher education and development for the past 25 years in many different locations around the world. In short, these scenarios are representative of extensive notes I have accumulated over my years as a teacher educator. Reflective questions which follow each scenario allow the reader to reflect on the issue in their own teaching contexts. Language teachers alone or working in groups can explore the many possible solutions to each scenario. Although reflective questions are provided at the end of each scenario, readers should also decide how they would explore each situation and what reflective tools would be most suitable to reflect on each scenario. I hope you enjoy reading and reflecting on the contents of *Reflective Language Teaching: From Research to Practice* as much as I have enjoyed writing the book.

Acknowledgements

The contents of this book come from my personal and professional reflections as a foreign language teacher over the past 24 years. However, it would not have been possible without the help and guidance of many people I encountered along the way in various institutions in which I worked around the world, but in particular my most recent encounter with Jack Richards who showed me how to write such a book and also for his contributions to the chapter on teachers' language proficiency. As always none of the contents of this book would have been possible without the support of my family who continue to guide my own reflections, so thank you Mija, Sarah and Ann. I would like to thank my colleague and good friend George Jacobs and also Dr Steve Mann for their invaluable insights and comments on drafts of this manuscript. Thanks also to Jenny Lovell whose support and guidance as a gentle editor at Continuum Press is most refreshing in such a profit-driven business world.

Reflective language teaching

Chapter Outline

Reflective teaching   2
    Origins of reflective teaching   2
    Definitions of reflective teaching   3
    Types of reflective teaching   4
    Levels of reflective teaching   6
    Benefits of reflective teaching   7
    Reflective teaching and professional development   7
Reflective language teaching   8
Reflection   11
Conclusion   12

Introduction

One day a young girl was watching her mother cooking a roast of beef. Just before the mother put the roast in the pot, she cut a slice off the end. The ever observant daughter asked her mother why she had done that, and the mother responded that her grandmother had always done it. Later that same afternoon, the mother was curious, so she called her mother and asked her the same question. Her mother, the child's grandmother, said that in her day she had to trim the roasts because they were usually too big for a regular pot.

This adapted story is relevant for language teachers in that teaching without any reflection, such as the nonreflecting child's mother when dealing with the routine of cutting the slice off the roast each time before she put it in the pot, shows that experience is not enough for effective teaching, for we do not learn much from experience alone as much as we learn from reflecting on that experience. Such continuous repetitive actions can also lead to burnout on any job. Dewey (1933) noted that teachers who do not bother to reflect on their work become slaves to routine (such as the mother in the above story) and their actions are guided mostly by impulse, tradition and/or authority rather than by informed decision making. This decision making, Dewey (1933) insisted should be based on systematic and conscious reflections because teaching experience when combined with these reflections can only lead to awareness, development and growth. More recently, Zeichner and Liston (1987: 24) returned to Dewey's original ideas when they distinguished between routine action and reflective action and suggested that for teachers 'routine action is guided primarily by tradition, external authority and circumstance' whereas reflective action 'entails the active, persistent and careful consideration of any belief or supposed form of knowledge'. One of the only ways for teachers to identify routine, and thus help counteract the possible burnout, is to engage in reflective teaching. When teachers reflect on their teaching, generally they take the time to stop and think about what is happening in their practice to make sense of it so that they can learn from their professional experiences. This introductory first chapter provides a brief background to the origins of reflective teaching, explains what reflective teaching is, and then outlines and describes what reflecting language teaching is for second language teachers.

Reflective teaching

Origins of reflective teaching

Many years ago Dewey (1933: 9) called for teachers to take reflective action that entails 'active, persistent, and careful consideration of any belief or supposed form of knowledge in light of the grounds that support it and the further consequences to which it leads'. Dewey (1933) identified three attributes of reflective individuals that I think are still important today for teachers: open-mindedness, responsibility and wholeheartedness. Open-mindedness is a desire to listen to more than one side of an issue and to give attention to alternative views. Responsibility means careful consideration of the consequences to which an action leads. Wholeheartedness implies that teachers can overcome fears and uncertainties to critically evaluate their practice in order to make meaningful change. The education community did not really hear about reflective teaching again until the early 1980s and it was not until the last 25 years that research interest in reflective teaching proliferated with the work of such educators as Donald Schön (1983, 1987). This renewed interest in reflective teaching was also due a press for the empowerment of teachers and out of the need to find some way to counteract a resurgence of teacher burnout in the teaching profession. At that time Schön's (1983) work centred on the notion of practitioner-generated intuitive practice. For Schön (1983, 1987), when a practitioner is confronted with a problem, he or she identifies the problem as being of a particular type and then applies an appropriate technique to solve the problem. However, he also asks what happens if these problems are nonroutine problems. In this case Schön says that practitioners engage in a process of problem setting rather than problem solving. Clarke (1995: 245) explains this process of problem setting as follows:

> When confronted by non-routine problems, skilled practitioners learn to conduct frame experiments in which they impose a kind of coherence on 'messy' situations. They come to new understandings of situations and new possibilities for action through a spiraling process of framing and reframing. Through the effects of a particular action, both intended and unintended, the situation 'talks back'. This conversation between the practitioner and the setting provides the data which may then lead to new meanings, further reframing, and plans for further action.

In recent times, reflective teaching has become something of a buzzword and is promoted in most teacher education and development programmes worldwide and most educators agree that some form of reflection is desirable for all teachers.

Definitions of reflective teaching

Today, one can find many different definitions of reflective teaching. However, most of the definitions can be contained within two main stances to reflective teaching, one that emphasizes reflection only on classroom actions, while the other also includes reflections on matters outside the classroom. Concerning the former approach, Cruickshank and Applegate (1981: 553) have characterized this reflection as a process that 'help[s] teachers to think about what happened, why it happened, and what else could have been done to reach their goals'. Schulman (1987: 19) concurred and suggested that reflection happens when a teacher 'reconstructs, reenacts and/or recaptures the events, emotions, and the accomplishments' of his or her teaching. However, Zeichner and Liston (1996) maintain that these definitions excluded the issue of linking teaching to the larger community called critical reflection. For Jay and Johnson (2002: 80) such critical reflection involves the broader historical, sociopolitical and moral context of schooling so that reflective teachers can 'come to see themselves as agents of change'. Within this latter definition then, if teachers want to reflect on student performance in their classes for example, they should not only consider the perspectives of the obvious main players (the teacher, the student and the parents), but also the school culture that includes the context in which the schooling is taking place. Because of these two very different approaches to reflective teaching, it is necessary for *each* teacher to define for themselves the concept of reflective teaching.

Types of reflective teaching

There are said to be three major types, or moments, of reflective practice where teachers can undertake reflection. The first moment happens during the event, such as classroom teaching and is called reflection-in-action. The second moment is thinking about the event after it has happened and this is called reflection-on-action. While the third moment is where teachers think about future actions and this is called reflection-for-action.

1. *Reflection-in-action*: The first type, of reflection-in-action (Schön 1983, 1987), happens when teachers take for granted their tacit knowledge of teaching because many of their actions have become routine while teaching. In order for teachers to carry out these routine actions they must employ a kind of knowing-in-action (Schön 1983). According to Schön, knowing-in-action is crucial for teachers because they cannot constantly question every action or reaction while they teach otherwise they would not be able to get through a class. So a teacher's knowing-in-action works similar to when we recognize a face in a crowd but we do not list or try to consciously piece together each separate facial feature that makes a person recognizable to us. We do not consciously think, 'Could that be. . . ?' – we just know. In addition, if you were asked to describe the features that prompted this recognition, it might be difficult because, as Schön (1983) has pointed out, that type of information usually remains at the subconscious level of our thoughts. However, when a new situation or event occurs and our established routines do not work for us, then according to Schön (1983), teachers use

reflection-in-action to cope. There is a sequence of moments in a process of reflection-in-action:

a. A situation develops which triggers spontaneous, routine responses (such as in knowing-in-action): for example, a student cannot answer a question about a topic he or she has explained in great detail during the previous class such as identifying a grammar structure.

b. Routine responses by the teacher (i.e., what the teacher has always done) do not produce a routine response and instead produce a surprise for the teacher: the teacher starts to explain how the student had already explained this grammar structure in the previous class and that this current silence is troubling for the teacher. Suddenly the student begins to cry.

c. This surprise response gets the teacher's attention and leads to reflection within an action: the teacher reacts quickly to try to find out why the student is suddenly crying by questioning the student or asking the student's classmates why they think the student is crying.

d. Reflection now gives rise to on-the-spot experimentation by the teacher: the student may or may not explain why he or she is crying. The teacher will take some measures (depending on the reaction or non reaction) to help solve the problem: ignore the situation, empathize with the student, help the student answer the question by modelling answers, and so forth.

According to Schön these sequences of moments are all present and lead to reflection-in-action. Experienced teachers can use their repertoire of teaching routines to experiment in order to solve the dilemma, but novice teachers may have a problem reflecting-in-action because they have not built up such an advanced schema of teaching routines.

2. *Reflection-on-action*: The second type of reflection is called reflection-on-action and involves thinking back on what was done to discover how knowing-in-action may have contributed to an unexpected action (Hatton and Smith, 1995). Here, teachers reflect on their classes after they have finished. Reflection-on-action focuses on the cognitive processes of teaching that depends on retrospection for analysis. So, reflection-on-action would come to mean some kind of metacognitive action, while reflection-in-action is the ability to frame problems based on past experiences, a type of conversation that takes place between the practitioner and an uncertain situation at the time of the occurrence of that situation.

3. *Reflection-for-action*: The third type of reflection is called reflection-for-action. Reflection-for-action is different from the previous types of reflection in that it is proactive in nature. Killon and Todnew (1991: 15) argue that reflection-for-action is the desired outcome of both previous types of reflection; they say that 'we undertake reflection, not so much to revisit the past or to become aware of the metacognitive process one is experiencing (both noble reasons in themselves) but to guide future action (the more practical purpose)'. Teachers can prepare for the future by using knowledge from what happened during class and what they reflected on after class.

As Stanley (1998:585) suggests, all three above is what 'reflective practitioners do when they look at their work in the moment (reflect-in-action) or in retrospect (reflect-on-action) in order to examine the reasons and beliefs underlying their actions and generate alternative actions for the future'.

Levels of reflective teaching

Connected to the different types of reflection outlined above is Day's (1993) notion of teachers acting within three different hierarchical levels of reflection: the first is where teachers focus their reflections on behavioural actions (**P1**), the second (**P2**) is where teachers also include justifications of these reflections based on current theories of teaching, while at the third level (**P3**) teachers include the first two and look beyond theories and practices to examine their meaning within ethical, moral and social ramifications. P1 is where teachers reflect at the level of classroom actions, the reasons for these actions are at P2, and justification for the work itself is at the level of P3. Day (1993) maintains that most teachers will find themselves planning and acting (constructing practice) at the P1 level and less on observation and reflection (deconstructing practice) at levels P2 and P3; in addition any change that may occur as a result of reflection happens mainly at the P1 action level. Day (1993) also criticizes Schön's (1983) notion of reflective practice (outlined above) because he says Schön fails to deal with discourse; he says that the dialogical dimension of learning can only emerge from the process of confrontation and reconstruction. Day's (1993) main point here is that reflection needs to be analytic and involve dialogue with others. Chapter 10 on teacher development groups outlines how teachers can use dialogue in a collaborative group manner in order to facilitate an individual teacher's reflection.

Benefits of reflective teaching

Why should language teachers look at what is and reflect on their work beyond the quick after-class muse of 'That was a good class' or 'The students were not very responsive today'? While these reflections are a necessary start, they are not very productive in that we do not know why the class was a good one (or even if the students learned anything or enjoyed it). Likewise, we should find out why the students were not responsive – it could be that the teacher was at fault, the time of day was not conducive to having a class (after lunch or 5pm on a Friday), or a host of many other possible and complex reasons. We need to know equally why a class was responsive or not responsive. We need to know what teachers believe to be good and bad teaching as well as what teachers do in their classrooms in order to be able to discuss teaching beyond mere preconceptions of what good teaching is or is not. Reflective teaching benefits teachers in the following ways:

- It frees the teacher from routine and impulsive action.
- It helps teachers become more confident in their actions and decisions.
- It provides information for teachers to make informed decisions.
- It helps teachers to critically reflect on all aspects of their work.
- It helps teachers to develop strategies for intervention and change.
- It recognizes teachers are professionals.
- It is a cathartic experience for practising (and novice) teachers.

Reflective teaching and professional development

Reflective teaching as it is discussed throughout this book differs from traditional professional development in that traditional professional development assumes that teachers can (or should) improve their classroom practices as a result of gaining new information and knowledge from taking a workshop or course. This top-down approach relies on the applications of research conducted by others as a framework for teaching and assumes that the transmission of knowledge (usually from an outside expert) in a workshop or the like will change classroom teaching behaviours. In reality though workshop sessions of this nature have little actual effect on classroom teaching as not much change happens and if it does, it does not last long. Reflective teaching as outlined in this book, although it shares the common goal of improving teaching, also provides for teachers changing their level of awareness of their current practices so that they can articulate their current practices. So this reflection can result in affirming current practices rather than making any behavioural teaching changes. Awareness of current practices is very important because as Freeman (1989: 33) says, 'one acts on or responds to the aspects of a situation of which one is aware'. Thus, reflective teaching involves looking at what is happening now in a teacher's life rather than ingesting new information or knowledge about teaching methods or assessment (although this too can aid a teacher's reflections).

Reflective language teaching

Language education embraced reflective teaching later than other areas within education and it is now considered an essential part of many language teacher education programmes worldwide. Pennington (1992: 51) first proposed a general reflective/developmental orientation for language teachers 'as a means for (1) improving classroom processes and outcomes, and (2) developing confident, self-motivated teachers and learners'. She described reflection for language teachers generally as 'deliberating on experience, and that of mirroring experience' and she also related teacher development to reflection where she maintained 'reflection is viewed as the input for development while also reflection is viewed as the output of development' (Pennington, 1992: 47). The focus here is on analysis, feedback and adaptation as an ongoing and recursive cycle in the classroom. However, and as in general education programmes, the precise definition of reflective language teaching remains vague (Roberts, 1998). For example, in its weakest version, reflective language teaching is said to be no more than thoughtful practice where teachers sometimes, as Wallace (1996: 292) suggests, 'informally evaluate various aspects of their professional expertise'. This type of informal reflection does not really lead to improved teaching and can even lead to more 'unpleasant emotions without suggesting any way forward' (Wallace, 1996: 13). A second stronger version of reflective language teaching proposes that teachers systematically reflect on their own teaching so that they take more responsibility for the actions they take in their classrooms. Richards and Lockhart (1994: 1) emphasize this version when they say that teachers should 'collect data about their teaching, examine their attitudes, beliefs, assumptions, and teaching practices, and use the information obtained as a basis for critical reflection about teaching'. Richards (1990: 5) maintains that such type of self-inquiry and critical thinking can 'help teachers move from a level where they may be guided largely by impulse, intuition, or routine, to a level where their actions are guided by reflection and critical thinking'. The contents of this book embrace the latter stronger version of reflective language teaching where there is conscious recall and examination of the classroom experiences as a basis for evaluation and decision-making and as a source for planning and action. In addition and for the purposes of this book, I use the terms reflection, reflective practice, reflective inquiry, reflective thinking and reflective teaching interchangeably indicating they hold the same meaning.

Reflective language teaching, as it is discussed in this book, is a bottom-up approach to teacher professional development that is based on the belief that experienced and novice language teachers can improve their understanding of their own teaching by consciously and systematically reflecting on their teaching experiences. It starts with the internal rather than the external and the real centre of the process is teaching itself, and it uses the teacher's actual teaching experiences as a basis for reflection. By making systematic reflections on teaching, teachers can become free from making too many impulsive decisions about what to teach, when to teach and why to teach it. Teachers should move beyond designing routine activities for their students to complete just because they have always done these. Reflective teaching enables teachers to act in a more deliberate and intentional manner.

Reflective practice means that teachers must subject their own beliefs of teaching and learning to *critical* examination, by articulating these beliefs and comparing these beliefs to their actual classroom practices to see if there are any contradictions between practice and underlying beliefs. Hatton and Smith (1995: 35) note however, that the term *critical* as used in critical reflection 'like reflection itself appears to be used loosely, some taking it to mean more than constructive self-criticism of one's actions with a view to improvement'. For example, in language teaching Pennington (1995: 706) has defined critical reflection as 'the process of information gained through innovation in relation to the teacher's existing schema for teaching' but does not include the broader society in her definition of critical reflection. However, Bartlett (1990: 204) sees a need to include the broader society in any definition of critical reflection within language teaching. He says that in order for language teachers to become critically reflective, they have to 'transcend the technicalities of teaching and think beyond the need to improve our instructional techniques'. For the purposes of this book the term critical in teaching includes 'making judgments about whether professional activity is equitable, just, and respectful of persons or not' (Hatton and Smith, 1995: 35). In addition, a language teacher is considered to be reflective when he or she seeks answers to the following questions:

1. What is he/she doing in the classroom (**method**)?
2. Why is he/she doing this (**reason**)?
3. What is the **result**?
4. Will he/she change anything based on the information gathered from answering the first two questions (**justification**)?

In order to answer the first question posed above teachers must first decide on what topic they want to reflect and then systematically gather data about that topic. Topics that teachers can choose from to critically reflect on include:

- Aspects of their life and work by engaging in self-reflection (Chapter 2).
- Their beliefs and classroom practices (Chapter 3).
- Critical incidents and case analysis in their teaching and careers (Chapter 4).
- Their language proficiency (Chapter 5).
- Their use of metaphors and maxims (Chapter 6).
- Communication and interaction in their classrooms (Chapter 7).

There are a number of procedures teachers can choose to facilitate this reflection over the course of their professional careers. Each procedure can be used alone or in combination with other procedures depending on the topic of investigation. For example, teachers can:

- Conduct an action research project to bring about change (Chapter 8).
- Write accounts of their experiences in teaching journals (Chapter 9).
- Join other teachers to discuss their teaching in teacher development groups (Chapter 10).
- Engage in classroom observations (individual, pairs, groups) (Chapter 11).
- Form critical friendships in team teaching or peer coaching arrangements (Chapter 12).
- Use concept mapping to focus their reflections (Chapter 13).

Much of the discussion of reflective teaching thus far assumes a positive relationship between reflective language teaching and teacher effectiveness. However, education has a long but disappointing history of attempts to relate personality variables, styles or qualities in teachers to student learning outcomes. Consequently, reflection and reflective practice has not escaped from its share of criticism. For example, a number of scholars have urged caution as to the applicability of reflective practice to real classroom situations. Some researchers have suggested that reflection and teaching are incompatible; reflection would paralyse a teacher from action and result in a dysfunctional classroom. Stanley (1998: 587) has cautioned language teachers that when they engage in reflective teaching, they may have some 'emotional reactions to what is uncovered through investigation'. Consequently, teachers should be emotionally ready to face what they may discover after they begin their reflections. Hoover (1994: 83) also wondered that: 'The promising acclamation about reflection has yielded little research qualitatively or quantitatively'. He did not however, rule out reflection in teaching but says reflection is a learned activity; he says it is 'a carefully planned set of experiences that foster a sensitivity to ways of looking at and talking about previously unarticulated beliefs concerning teaching' (Hoover, 1994: 84). He also says that this self-analysis requires time and opportunity. The contents of this book are research-informed throughout (and much of this research is my own) and the various opportunities I outline for teachers to use when reflecting on their work are based on the results of this research and thus is one attempt at addressing Hoover's (1994) concerns with the concept of reflective teaching. There still remain some unanswered questions about reflective teaching however, that teachers may want to consider as they reflect (adapted from Hatton and Smith, 1994: 34–6). These are:

1. Is reflection limited to thought processes about action, or more bound up in the action itself?
2. Is reflection immediate and short term, or more extended and systematic?
3. Is reflection problem-centred, finding solutions to real classroom problems, or not?
4. How critical does one get when reflecting?

Reflection

➤ Are you a reflective teacher? How do you know?
➤ What kind of reflections do you do immediately before and after teaching a language class?
➤ Do you reflect during class? If yes, how do you do this?
➤ What is your definition of reflective practice?
➤ Compare your definition with the definition of other teachers. Can you see any patterns in the different definitions (if they are different)?

➤ What is critical reflection and how is it different from reflection?

➤ Dewey mentioned the following dispositions of a reflective practitioner: *open-mindedness, responsibility* and *wholeheartedness.* What is your understanding of each of these?

➤ Which type or moment of reflective practice (from the three types outlined above) would be most difficult for you to implement? Why?

➤ How can experienced teachers perform reflection-in-action as they teach?

➤ How can reflecting-in-action and reflecting-on-action lead to reflecting-for-action?

➤ Detail one of your reflection-in-action moments as outlined in the steps discussed above in reflection-in-action

➤ Which level of reflection do you think you are operating at P1, P2 or P3? How do you know?

➤ Do you think it is worth it to reflect on your practice even if you do not discover new teaching or assessment methods and just gain a better understanding of what you are doing now? Explain.

➤ How would you attempt to answer each of the four questions on the method, reason, result and justification for your teaching decisions posed above?

➤ Which question would be most difficult for you to answer and why?

➤ How do you think method, reason, result, justification are all interrelated?

➤ Try to answer the four questions posed by Hatton and Smith above.

➤ Oberg and Blades (1990: 179) maintain that the potential of being reflective 'lies not in the theory it allows us to develop (about practice or reflection) but the evolution of ourselves as a teacher. It's focus is life; we continually return to our place of origin, but it is not the place we left'. What is your understanding of this statement?

➤ Do you think it is unreasonable to expect language teachers consistently to engage in reflection? If no, why not?

➤ If yes, how often should teachers engage in reflection?

➤ Why do you think teachers should reflect on their practice?

Conclusion

Reflection for teachers as it is outlined in this introduction (and indeed the book) is much more than taking a few minutes to think about how to keep students on task. Reflective language teaching involves teachers systematically gathering data about their teaching and using this information to make informed decisions about their practice. It thus implies a dynamic way of being in the classroom. I suggest this book not be read as a prescription for reflection; rather, individual, and groups of, teachers should build on what is presented in the book and generate further examples of principles and practices of reflection that best suit their particular situations and contexts.

2 Self-reflection

Chapter Outline

Introduction

Over the centuries we have been encouraged to observe our lives so that we can better understand who we are; Buddha, for example, emphasized direct experience of reality to bring about greater insight into our lives while the great philosopher Socrates is remembered for his famous quote: 'The unexamined life is not worth living'. This is an important saying too for experienced language teachers because self-reflection defined in this chapter as 'the condition of consciousness characterized by awareness, objectivity, clarity, acceptance and being in the present as well as by absence of opinion, preference, prejudice, and attachment' (Bergsgaard and Ellis, 2002: 56), is an essential beginning point for teachers before they explore other aspects of their work. As Palmer (1998: 3) suggests: 'The work required to "know thyself" is neither selfish nor narcissistic. Whatever self-knowledge we attain as teachers will serve our students and our scholarship well. Good teaching requires self-knowledge; it is a secret hidden in plain sight'. This chapter outlines how teachers can begin their self-reflections by telling their story: where they came from, where they are now and ultimately where they may want to go through the use of story telling and by compiling a teaching portfolio.

What the research says

Palmer (1998: 2) has observed that some teachers can lose heart over the years because teaching becomes a 'daily exercise in vulnerability' for them. Because teachers are constantly in the public eye, they tend to try hard to keep their private identity hidden so as to reduce this vulnerability. As such, Palmer (1998: 2) maintains that over the years teachers build up a wall between their inner selves and outer performances and so he suggests it is important for all teachers to 'attend to the inner teacher to cultivate a sense of identity and integrity'. Johnson and Golombek (2002: 6) maintain that language teachers can also make sense of their experiences through telling their stories of their professional development 'within their own professional worlds'. By telling their stories, language teachers can 'impose order and coherence on unpredictable classroom reality where there are always alternative solutions to cope with similar problems' (Olshtain and Kupferberg, 1998: 187). Palmer (1998: 5) urges all teachers regardless of the subject matter they teach to "ask the 'who'" question – who is the self that teaches?'. Research suggests that when teachers engage in personal self-reflection they can:

- recall previous experiences for self-discovery
- become more aware of who they are as teachers
- become more aware of how they got to where they are at present
- become more aware of what they have accomplished over their career
- decide what is important for them personally and professionally
- become more aware of their thoughts actions and feelings

- decide where they may want to go in the future both personally and professionally
- gain keen insight into themselves and their practice
- share with other teachers a strong sense of personal identity that infuses their work.

Another way practising language teachers can take stock of themselves and what they have accomplished over their years of teaching is by constructing a teaching portfolio. Brown and Wolfe-Quintero (1997: 28) maintain that a teaching portfolio 'tells the story of a teacher's efforts, skills, abilities, achievements and contributions to his/her colleagues, institution, academic discipline or community'. A teaching portfolio is a collection of any aspect of a teacher's work that tells the story of the teacher's efforts, skills, abilities, achievements and contributions to his or her students, colleagues, institution, academic discipline or community (Richards and Farrell, 2005). Farrell (2002) suggests three main types of teaching portfolios that practising teachers can compile: a *Working Portfolio* in order to document growth and development towards some performance standards that may have been set within the institution, or district, or at the national level. The materials that are included in this portfolio are intended to reflect a work-in-progress and growth over time and not intended to be polished documents. The second is a *Showcase Portfolio* which showcases documents that highlight a teacher's best work and accomplishments. The third is a *Critical Incident Portfolio* and documents selected incidents (see also Chapter 4) that were particularly provocative and illuminating to teachers. The teacher should include a caption that explains the rationale for choosing the topic and a reflective statement about the critical incident. In this way, the teacher can outline his or her underlying philosophy of teaching and learning languages. Farrell (2002) discovered that the very process of compiling, developing and analysing a teaching portfolio helps teachers see their professional strengths all in one location. Research suggests that compiling teaching portfolios can benefit language teachers in the following ways:

- it cultivates reflection and self-assessment
- it provides self-renewal
- it promotes collaboration
- it encourages ownership and empowerment
- it shows a teacher's efforts, skills, abilities, achievements and contributions.

Case study: self-reflection with the 'Tree of Life'

The case study reported in this chapter uses the *Tree of Life* (Merryfield, 1993) as a self-reflective tool that briefly outlines this author's personal and professional journey as outlined in a graphic representation in Figure 2. The 'Tree of Life' is a reflective tool for trainee teachers and it is divided into the *roots*, or early influences, the *trunk*, later influences, and the limbs, the most recent influences

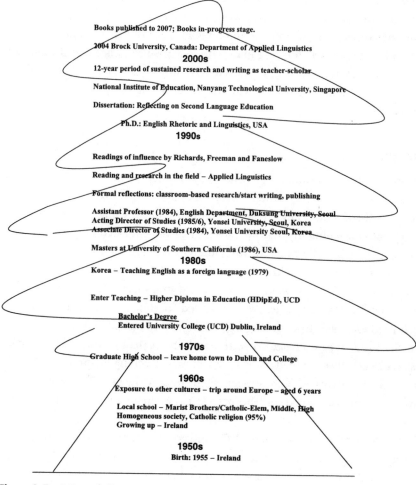

Books published to 2007; Books in-progress stage.

2004 Brock University, Canada: Department of Applied Linguistics

2000s

12-year period of sustained research and writing as teacher-scholar

National Institute of Education, Nanyang Technological University, Singapore

Dissertation: Reflecting on Second Language Education

Ph.D.: English Rhetoric and Linguistics, USA

1990s

Readings of influence by Richards, Freeman and Faneslow

Reading and research in the field – Applied Linguistics

Formal reflections: classroom-based research/start writing, publishing

Assistant Professor (1984), English Department, Duksung University, Seoul
Acting Director of Studies (1985/6), Yonsei University, Seoul, Korea
Associate Director of Studies (1984), Yonsei University Seoul, Korea

Masters at University of Southern California (1986), USA

1980s

Korea – Teaching English as a foreign language (1979)

Enter Teaching – Higher Diploma in Education (HDipEd), UCD

Bachelor's Degree
Entered University College (UCD) Dublin, Ireland

1970s

Graduate High School – leave home town to Dublin and College

1960s

Exposure to other cultures – trip around Europe – aged 6 years

Local school – Marist Brothers/Catholic-Elem, Middle, High
Homogeneous society, Catholic religion (95%)
Growing up – Ireland

1950s

Birth: 1955 – Ireland

Figure 2 Tom's Tree of Life

especially as each limb represents an important or critical incident in one's life. I present this reflection by first briefly focusing on the 'roots' and the 'trunk' and then I look at the 'limbs' of the tree that show the experiences that brought me to where I am as I write this book which is explained in *current limb*.

Roots

The roots of my tree of life include my family values, early experiences and my heritage. As can be seen in my Tree of Life my upbringing in a small town in Ireland was typical for my generation: homogeneous in class (middle), race and religion (Catholic). One of the important early influences in my life was a trip to Spain and France when I was 6 years old and an amusing incident on the trip consisted of my mother and myself being lost in Spain and using a lot of body language when trying to explain to a Spanish policeman the location of the hotel we were staying at. I was to have similar experiences in the Middle East and throughout Asia when I arrived to teach English as a foreign language in 1978/9.

Trunk

From childhood through high school, the influences that were to shape me as a teacher and teacher-scholar were sometimes reactionary. For example, I decided that I would never teach the way many of my grade school teachers went about teaching me. For the most part, I was educated in the teacher-led classes, but especially while learning foreign languages and English language. In English class we would read aloud and not have any idea what the text was about. In Spanish class we memorized grammar rules but never practised speaking the language. We memorized vocabulary and wrote essays that followed formulas. In Irish language class we were punished if we did not fill-in-the-blank-type exercises correctly (with the correct grammar test item). I was consistently reminded of the failure of these teaching methods by frequent trips to Europe with my family made when I noticed the ease of communication young German or Dutch students my age had when interacting in English with me.

University life in Ireland in the 1970s did not change my views much and after doing my degree I went into teaching. I had no real opinion about my career move until my first week in a secondary school during my teaching practice. After my Bachelor's Degree, I studied for a Higher Diploma in Education

(H. Dip. in Ed.) at University College Dublin, Ireland that had as one of its requirements, practice teaching for four hours per week in a secondary school for each week of the academic year. I was placed in a typical neighbourhood school in south Dublin. One incident in class early in the year made me reflect on my own educational experiences and the reactionary mode I was to take as a teacher and (teacher-scholar later) at that time (1977).

I was teaching a first year secondary class in Business English and one of the students (male, 13 years old) questioned my reasons for making them participate in a class activity. At first, I was angry that he should question me in the manner he did (shouted out to the class) and so I made him write me a letter of apology after I had silenced him. After reflecting and reading the letter, I realized that I was just repeating what my high school teachers had done to me: silencing any opinions different from the teacher's. I changed my approach to my students' opinions after that incident and have tried to really listen to them ever since. Sometimes I am successful, while at other times I may still not listen clearly – I have become more successful I think in recent times and I always try to put myself in students' shoes before I react.

Another series of incidents that were to influence my approach to classroom observation as a language teacher-educator (especially later while teaching in a university in Singapore) occurred during the same practicum experience (Farrell, 1996). As a student teacher I was supposed to be observed and evaluated three or four times during the year by a supervisor/teacher-educator from the university. I was actually observed teaching three times during the academic year and each time I became progressively more nervous while teaching during those observed classes but did not know why. I realize now that having had no pre-observation discussion (the supervisor was already in the classroom each time seated at the back of the room giving me 'The Look' of the expert: 'Show me what you can do'), and having no post-observation conference added to fuel my anxiety. My only feedback was my evaluation by way of the final grade (pass) sheet at the end of the year.

Limbs

Each limb of the tree represents an experience or a critical incident that modified my view as a language educator and my approach to language teacher education. What follows is an account of how these incidents and books/papers influenced my own development as a language teacher and teacher-scholar as I call myself now.

Language teacher

Several incidents occurred in my professional career that shaped me both as a language educator and a teacher-scholar. Space, however, dictates that I can only choose a few. The first important incident was my development as a foreign language educator in Korea. My initial readings in a very new field called TESOL (Teaching English to speakers of other languages) and Applied Linguistics brought me under the influence of Steven Krashen (1981, 1982). I read these from a language educator practitioner point of view as I wanted to be able to directly apply principles or theories to my teaching. I found myself in a survival mode in Korea once again in the sense that the context and culture were both very new to me. At this stage of my development as a language educator I realized my theories were coming from my practice which is fine because as Bullough (1997: 20) says: 'unless theories come from practice, they will not apply to practice'. Also, I noticed that most of the research and content in the field of teaching second or foreign language education in the 1970s was under the influence of the field of Applied Linguistics, itself a very young field; topics such as Error Analysis, Second Language Acquisition, Syllabus Design (especially the Functional/Notional Approach) and the like influenced my practice and reflections. But I found Krashen's work most seductive at this time in my professional career because I realized that I could make my own classroom applications.

It was then, in 1986, that I really started to reflect on my practice and to question these earlier scientific/research conceptions of second language acquisition (SLA) that I seemed to favour and also the theory/values-based conception of the communicative approaches that were just appearing in the field. I realized that I was moving into a more art/craft approach when I conceptualized my practice approach (Freeman and Richards, 1993); this to me was a process where my context in general and my classroom in particular were most important in terms of creating an effective learning environment. I thus began to look at all aspects of my professional life. The work that influenced my thinking and many of these workshops (on the use of video; testing; the place of grammar; group work) was by John Fanselow. Fanselow (1987, 1988, 1992) takes the approach that teachers should be responsible for their own classrooms, and thus he encourages teachers to explore their classroom practice from the point of view of analysing the communication patterns that occur in it. This reflective curiosity brought me back to graduate school in the USA and a Ph.D. This intense period of reflection let me to write a dissertation on the topic of reflective practice and I have been researching, presenting workshops, publishing papers and books ever since as a teacher-scholar.

Teacher-scholar

Actually I first became a teacher-scholar because of an appointment as Director of English as a foreign language programmes in Yonsei University, Seoul, Korea. However, prior to that appointment, I was a director of a language centre at the university where I was teaching. At this centre I was not involved in teacher training or education. I was in charge of placing students at their correct level of English proficiency in the centre and finding teachers to teach them. As director of all the foreign language programmes at the next university for a period of three years, I gave many workshops to the teachers on various topics of teaching foreign language, professional development and I developed course syllabi for all the 24 part-time, non-native teachers in these foreign language programmes. As this was taking place in the late 1980s I began to read in the field again and was interested to see a change of direction away from hard-core Linguistics as a guiding light to the field, to more recognition of second language teacher education, teachers and teaching itself. Freeman (1989: 17) best expressed what I was thinking at that time when he said that TESOL was 'fragmented and unfocused due to the different disciplines competing for control: Applied Linguistics, Methodology, SLA, while overlooking the core, teaching'. He acknowledged that they all contribute to teaching but are ancillary to it and as such should not be the primary subject matter of second language teacher education. In other words, I was fully motivated to devote my career to developing TESOL as a field in its own right.

One of the highlights of my teacher-scholar career occurred while I was in Singapore and that was when I had the good fortune to meet and work with Dr Jack Richards, one of the preeminent scholars in the field of second language teacher education and development. I was extremely fortunate to have had the opportunity of working with him on the topic of professional development for language teachers that led to coauthoring a book on this topic (see Richards and Farrell, 2005).

Current limb

My current 'limb' started when I arrived at Brock University, Ontario, Canada in July 2004 to take up a teaching position in the Department of Applied Linguistics where I have carried on from my previous appointments as a teacher-scholar in the area of Applied Linguistics and TESOL. I take a constructivist approach to my classes for I believe that all my students will make sense of the theories and ideas that I present in their own way. I agree with Williams and Burden (1997: 2) when they say that, 'Each individual constructs his or her own reality.' I believe my students have a personal framework of how languages are learned and should be taught before they come to Brock, and whatever theories they read about or hear about in classes are placed in light of their personal frameworks. In other words, I believe my students actively construct their own representations of teaching and try to assimilate any new theories into their prior beliefs. As Kaufman and Brooks (1996: 324) say 'Constructivist teachers look for and value the students' points of view'. I have developed the following principles that I hope will guide me for the future as a teacher-scholar:

- What all my students bring to my courses in the form of prior experiences and prior knowledge is very important to the educational experience and to me as a professor. I start all my courses at Brock (and many of my classes) trying to get the students to articulate these experiences. This can be done with reflective devices such as the 'Tree of Life' (as in this statement), life histories and metaphor analysis. I have also recently been funded by the Humanities Research Institute at Brock University to reflect on the impact of my graduate courses on my students' prior beliefs. I have nearly completed writing up the results of this project.
- Second Language Teacher Education and Applied Linguistics Programmes should provide students with the tools to reflect so that they can continue to develop as teachers after the teacher education course. This can be accomplished by collaborative assignments, observation (self, peer and group), case studies, action research, journal writing, teacher development groups, etc. and I have published journal articles on all of these topics. This book is a culmination of my research on the topic for the past 15 years (e.g. Farrell, 1996, 1998a, 1998b, 1998c, 1998d, 1998e, 1999a, 1999b, 1999c, 1999d, 2001a, 2001b, 2002, 2003, 2004a, 2004b, 2004c, 2006a, 2006b, 2006c, 2006d, 2006e, 2007a, 2007b, 2008).
- My research is dedicated to promoting reflective practice. I have and will continue to conduct workshops on the topic of reflective practice for language teachers inside and outside Canada.
- Each research participant is vitally important to me; therefore, my research designs all draw on qualitative techniques. This is because in the phenomenological, subjective sense, I cannot separate myself from this research as I am a part of the process.

Case study reflection

➤ Comment as you please on this author's journey so far.
➤ Fill in your Tree of Life to 'tell' your story.
➤ Write your story from this tree.
➤ Share your story with another language teacher and have that teacher share his or her story with you.

From research to practice

Teacher stories

Teachers can self-reflect on their practice by articulating their stories to themselves or others because these stories reveal the 'knowledge, ideas, perspectives, understandings, and experiences that guide their work' (Johnson and Golombek, 2002: 7). By telling their story teachers can make better sense of seemingly random experiences because they hold the inside knowledge, especially personal intuitive knowledge, expertise and experience that is based on their accumulated years as language educators teaching in schools and classrooms. These self-reflection stories can provide a rich source of teacher-generated information that allows them to reflect on how they got where they are today, how they conduct practice, the thinking and problem solving they employ during their practice, and their underlying assumptions, values and beliefs that have ruled their past and current practices. As Taggart and Wilson (1998: 164) maintain, teacher autobiographical sketches offer insight 'into the past to uncover preconceived theories about teaching and learning'. Once these stories have been told they can be analysed alone or with a peer (a critical friend) where the peer can give a different insight into the meaning and interpretation of the story than if the story was analysed alone.

Teacher portfolios

Language teachers can also 'tell' their story by compiling and reflecting on their teaching portfolio. Two metaphors, the *mirror* and the *map*, help best answer why language teachers should assemble a teaching portfolio. The *mirror* metaphor captures the reflective nature of a developmental portfolio as it allows teachers to 'see themselves' over time. The *map* metaphor symbolizes creating a plan and setting goals. After reviewing the evidence collected over time, teachers can reflect on where they were, where they are now, and, most importantly, where they want to go. A teaching portfolio might include lesson plans, anecdotal records, student projects, class newsletters, videotapes, annual evaluations and letters of recommendation. A teaching portfolio is not a one-time snapshot of where the teacher is at present; rather, it is an evolving collection of carefully selected professional experiences, thoughts and goals. This collection can be accompanied with the teacher's written (or oral) reflection and self-assessment of the collection itself and plans for the future. Teachers can put the following items in a teaching portfolio:

a. a teaching philosophy
b. description of teaching goals and responsibilities such as courses and assignments
c. materials developed by the teacher including lesson plans, syllabi, assignments and examinations
d. evidence of teaching performance and effectiveness from student and peer feedback

Language teaching is a multifaceted profession. Teachers do more than simply teach. Among other things, they are involved in planning instruction, regularly updating their knowledge on teaching, preparing teaching materials, collaborating with colleagues in different ways, assessing student learning as well as assessing their own teaching. Each of these kinds of activities is an important dimension of the teacher's work and in reviewing and planning his or her professional development, a teacher needs to look at his or her practice as a whole. A teaching portfolio is an excellent instrument for accomplishing this since it is a collection of documents and other items that provides information about different aspects of a teacher's work. Each teacher's portfolio will be different and my own has 75 double-sided pages (and thus impossible to include in this collection).

The following materials should be a part of any teaching portfolio regardless of the specific purpose for creating it (from Farrell, 2002):

1. *Knowledge of subject matter.* This first section of the teaching journal outlines what you know about the subject you teach and how this

impacts the classroom (context) you teach in. Documents that relate to your knowledge of the subject matter might include the following artefacts:

- Highlights of a unit of instruction, reflections on the class and implications for future instruction. Regarding future instruction for example, one language teacher may want to experiment with using an inductive approach to teaching grammar in designing lessons and assessments. Another teacher may want to think about performing some action research topics in their classes. Still another teacher may want to try out task-based learning with certain classes.
- A research paper (or other original materials such as books, papers, etc.) you wrote on the subject matter you teach and what you learned from the contents of the paper as it relates to your teaching. This shows that you are reflecting on the subject matter you teach.
- Descriptions of courses, or workshops you conducted.
- A reflective journal you have been keeping about your teaching of the subject matter.
- A reflective essay about how your knowledge of the subject matter has informed your instructional decisions and how you plan to increase student learning. For example, as a language teacher educator my reflective essay would include answers to the following questions about curriculum construction:
  a. How much of the curriculum of the course(s) you teach should be influenced by:

    - *Reality of the classroom?*
    - *What research suggests we should include?*
    - *What practising teachers think?*
    - *What trainee teachers think?*

  b. How was the curriculum of the course(s) you teach set – by whom and why?
  c. What is the impact (what conceptual changes did your students take on as a result of taking your course) of the curriculum in your course(s)?
  d. How did you investigate this?
  e. Do you know what aspects of your course(s) teachers are using/ implementing during their first year(s) as teachers?
  f. How did you investigate this?

   g. Do you think teachers who are in the schools/institutes now should be asked to help us when we are designing the curriculum of the methods courses?

2. *Planning, delivery and assessing instruction*: This section of the teaching portfolio reflects who you are as a teacher. Documents compiled for this section include a statement about your beliefs and values regarding language teaching and learning, what you do in the classroom (lesson plans, video of a class, student work examples), and what others think about your classroom work (supervisor's evaluation, peer observation reports):

   - A reflection of your beliefs about teaching and learning. This outlines your approach to teaching the language. For example, what are your conceptions of language teaching? Are you influenced by *Science/Research Conceptions, Theory/Values Conceptions* and/or *Art/Craft Conceptions* (see Freeman and Richards, 1993, for a discussion on this).
   - Sample lesson plans.
   - Samples of student work.
   - Samples of students' evaluations/feedback of your lessons.
   - A videotape and/or audiotape of you teaching a class with a written description of what you were teaching and your reflection on that class.
   - Feedback from a supervisor and/or an administrator.
   - Classroom observation report from a peer teacher.

3. *Professionalism*: This final section of the teaching portfolio shows who you are as a teacher in the wider community. Documents compiled for this section include a statement of your development plans are, and other documents that confirm your standing in the profession (résumé, copies of degrees, etc.):

   - A current professional development plan. This plan outlines what you plan to achieve professionally in the near future such as attending certain conferences, seminars and inservice courses that can upgrade one's skills, researching certain topics (action research projects) that can make one a more effective teacher and upgrading one's technical skills (e.g. IT).
   - A current résumé.
   - A list of membership of professional organizations.

- A description of any leadership positions held such as head of department, curriculum development unit and committees.
- Copies of degrees, certificates, honours and awards held.

Reflection

➤ Write your autobiographical sketch that outlines some of the realities, dilemmas, joys and rewards of your teaching life.

➤ Compare this with another teacher's sketch of his or her life story.

➤ Have you ever compiled a teaching portfolio? If so, what were the contents of the portfolio and how long did it take you to compile it?

➤ If not, try to compile your teaching portfolio by including suggested contents (a to d) above.

➤ Do you think it is useful for teachers to read each other's portfolios? What form of response would be useful when reading someone else's portfolio?

Conclusion

According to Bullough (1997: 19), telling one's story: 'Is a way of getting a handle on what we believe, on models, metaphors and images that underpin action and enable meaning making, on our theories. Through story telling, personal beliefs become explicit, and in being made explicit they can be changed, where change is warranted, and a new or different story results; we behold differently'. Self-reflection for language teachers as outlined in this chapter is really self-initiated, self-directed and self-evaluated because no one else can do this for us. In telling my story in this chapter and by reflecting on some critical incidences in my career, I have come to see some of the principles that have emerged from my practice. As Palmer (1998: 2) suggests, the very act of teaching holds a mirror to the soul for teachers, and he urges teachers to look into that mirror and 'not run from what I see, I have a chance to gain self-knowledge – and knowing myself is as crucial to good teaching as knowing my students and my subject'. So by telling their story and also compiling and reviewing a teaching portfolio for self-reflection, teachers can come to know themselves better and really appreciate how much they have accomplished and grown during their careers.

Chapter scenario

Paul, an instructor in an Intensive English Programme in the USA, teaches academic writing and advanced listening. He has kept a teaching portfolio for several years and includes many things in it such as his course outlines and course objectives, sample teaching materials, narrative journal entries that describe different issues he had to resolve during the semester; two lessons, student evaluations, a written account of two classroom observations by peers, and a reflective essay about his approach to teaching and his own teacher development. After he reviewed his teaching portfolio, Paul was pleasantly surprised at the breath and depth of what he had accomplished. Paul had the following comments to make about assembling a teaching portfolio: 'I really enjoyed putting my portfolio together. It reminded me of how far I have come as a teacher since I started teaching'. Paul was happy that he had compiled his teaching portfolio also because a new director was appointed and wanted to review the whole Intensive English Programme. Specifically, this new director wanted to know what each teacher had been involved in and with in the past such as the teacher's course outlines, lesson plans and other related information. When it was Paul's turn to be appraised by the new director, he simply took out his teaching portfolio and explained what he had compiled and why he had included it. The Director was very impressed, for as Paul noted: 'The Director's mouth opened when she saw my portfolio and how I had arranged everything. She told me that I was well prepared and came across as a professional teacher'.

Reflection

- Paul was proactive in compiling his teaching portfolio. What items in his teaching portfolio made him look like a professional teacher to his new director?
- Explain why compiling a teaching portfolio reminded Paul of 'how far' he had come as a teacher? What items in his teaching portfolio would show him this?
- What other items could he have included?

Teachers' beliefs and practices 3

Chapter Outline

Introduction

Teacher beliefs, defined as 'unconsciously held assumptions about students, classrooms, and the academic material to be taught' (Kagan, 1992: 65), are developed over a teacher's career and are said to influence a teacher's instructional decisions and actions. It is difficult to access what a teacher believes about teaching and learning except by asking that teacher. However, what teachers say they do (their espoused theories) and what they actually do in the classroom (their theories-in-action) are not always the same. In fact, a language teacher's espoused beliefs may be an unreliable guide to their actual classroom practices. This is especially important if there is any discrepancy between what teachers say they believe and their actual classroom practices. This chapter explores the complex issue of how language teachers can reflect on their espoused theories and beliefs and compare these to their theories-in-use so that they can become more aware of the influence of both.

What the research says

Borg (2003: 81) maintains that 'teachers are active, thinking decision-makers who make instructional choices by drawing on complex practically-oriented, personalized, and context-sensitive networks of knowledge, thoughts, and beliefs'. As a result teachers actively construct their theory of teaching by, among other things, reflecting on their beliefs systems and examining how these beliefs are translated (or not) into actual classroom practice (Tsui, 2003). Burns (1992: 59) investigated the influence of six experienced teachers' beliefs on instructional practice related to the use of written language in beginning ESL classrooms and identified 'an extremely complex and interrelated network of underlying beliefs . . . which appeared to influence the instructional practices and approaches adopted by the teachers'. Borg (1998), through a series of classroom observations and interviews, illustrated the manner in which the teacher's instructional judgements and decisions in teaching grammar were directly influenced by the interaction of his belief system, his educational and professional experiences, and the context of instruction. Knezedivc (2001: 10) has suggested that awareness of beliefs and practices is a necessary starting point in reflections because we cannot develop 'unless we are aware of who we are and what we do' and 'developing awareness is a process of reducing the discrepancy between what we do and what we think we do'.

A number of studies have sought to investigate the extent to which beliefs and practices converge or diverge. In an Asia-Pacific-wide study of writing teachers, Pennington *et al.* (1997: 131) discovered that a gap existed between ideal perceptions of teaching and actual teaching situations mainly because the participants explained that the 'constraints of the educational system' caused these gaps because the teachers adapted the 'process approach' to writing to suit their individual circumstances. Similarly, Richards, Gallo and Renandya (2001: 54) discovered that although many teachers stated they followed a communicative approach to teaching, 'many of the respondents still hold firmly to the belief that grammar is central to language learning and direct grammar teaching is needed by their EFL/ESL students'. A recent study by Breen *et al.* (2001: 497) examined the relationship between the classroom practices and beliefs of 18 teachers in Australia, individually and as a group, and discovered that even though individual teachers favoured distinctive practices unique to their particular classrooms, there was also the presence of 'a collective pedagogy' that the group as a whole shared. Consequently, research on language teacher beliefs has revealed the following:

- Teachers' beliefs influence perception and judgement.
- Teachers' beliefs play a role in how information on teaching is translated into classroom practices.
- What teachers say they do and what they actually do in their classes may not always be the same.
- Awareness of beliefs and practices is one necessary starting point in reflections.
- Awareness of the sources of teacher beliefs is important for self-reflection.
- Understanding teachers' beliefs is essential to improving teaching practices and teacher education programmes.
- Understanding teachers' beliefs about the language they are teaching is important.

Case study: beliefs and classroom practices of experienced grammar teachers

The case study reported in this chapter examined the beliefs of two experienced language teachers and their actual instructional practices while teaching grammar (Farrell and Lim, 2005). In addition, the study sought to examine how the stated beliefs corresponded to the observed classroom practices; whether they converged or diverged. The two teachers Velma and Daphne (both pseudonyms), were interviewed to obtain their stated beliefs, and also observed while teaching grammar classes.

Beliefs

Regarding the two teachers' beliefs about issues related to their teaching of grammar (as articulated during the interviews), both agreed that the teaching of grammar is crucial in order to enable students to use grammar structures correctly in their written work. Although the teachers said that their students may not need to be able to explain grammar rules explicitly, both agreed that the students should have the ability to apply these rules and structures correctly in sentences so that they would have fewer grammatical errors in their speech and in writing. Furthermore, Daphne said that she would not hesitate to directly re-teach a grammar structure by explicit means if she discovered that her students had not fully understood the structure and were not able to use it correctly in speech and writing.

Classroom practices

Regarding the two teachers' actual classroom practices when teaching English grammar, it was observed that both adopted a somewhat traditional approach to grammar teaching: teacher-centred, with both teaching grammar structures overtly with little integration of grammar into speaking and writing activities. In addition, during the classes that were observed, both Daphne and Velma used the metalanguage of grammar to explain grammar items. For example, Daphne used sentences such as: 'singular noun must have a singular verb', and Velma made reference to terms such as 'regular verbs' and 'irregular verbs'. Another similarity between the two teachers' classroom practices was the manner in which both provided feedback on their students' compositions. For example, the teachers marked each grammar error made by their students in the compositions and the correct version was then written above the error.

Case study reflection

➤ What is your opinion of the method the teachers' beliefs and practices about grammar teaching were explored?
➤ Can you think of other ways they could have been explored?
➤ What are your beliefs about teaching grammar?
➤ What are your classroom practices about teaching grammar?
➤ Are your beliefs about teaching grammar reflected in your classroom practices about teaching grammar? How do you know?
➤ One reason why teachers who may express enthusiasm for alternative methods of grammar instruction continue to employ the traditional approach to grammar teaching is the powerful emotions and attitudes

attached to traditional grammar teaching and learning. Can you explain this?

➤ Can you think of any other ways teaching beliefs and classroom practices can be investigated and compared than was discussed in the case study above?

From research to practice

One problem with examining teachers' beliefs is that they often remain hidden to the teacher and so must be brought to the level of awareness by being articulated in some way. When teachers are given a chance to articulate their beliefs about teaching and learning, they soon discover that their beliefs are far from simple. After articulating beliefs, teachers should then examine the sources of these beliefs that have been built up over a teacher's career. For example, Shi and Cumming's (1995: 104) study of the beliefs and practice of five experienced language teachers discovered that even though they had been educated in the same institution and by the same methods, the knowledge guiding their instruction is largely based on personal beliefs 'founded on years of previous experience, reflection, and information'. One or more of the following sources of beliefs can be considered and used either individually or in combination (adapted from Richards and Lockhart, 1994):

- *Teachers' past experience as students.* For example, if a teacher has learned a second language successfully and comfortably by memorizing vocabulary lists, then there is a good chance that the same teacher will have his or her students memorize vocabulary lists too.
- *Experience of what works best in their classes.* This may be the main source of beliefs about teaching for many second language teachers and as such many practising teachers may not want to break an established, and perceived successful, routine.
- *Established practice within a school.* These practices can be difficult to change because the school has always used this method or teachers would have to complete a particular unit in a specific time period.
- *Personality factors of teachers.* This can be an important source of beliefs as some teachers really enjoy conducting role-play or group work in their classes while others are more comfortable conducting traditional teacher-fronted lessons.

- *Educationally based or research-based principles.* This can also be a source of teachers' beliefs in that a teacher may draw on his or her understanding of research in second language reading to support use of predicting style exercises in reading classes.
- *Method-based sources of beliefs.* This suggest that teachers support and implement a particular method in their classes, as for example, when a teacher decides to use total physical response (TPR) to teach beginning second language learners, he or she is following a method of suspending early production of language for the learner.

In the case study reported on in this chapter, one of the teachers, Daphne, indicated that the source of her beliefs related to grammar teaching originated from her own experiences as a student in the school system, having herself experienced English language learning by explicit instruction on the rules of grammar. Now Daphne firmly believes that her students can also benefit from this overt approach to grammar teaching. However, both teachers also constantly spoke about how their teaching was constrained by time factors and so many of their classroom instructional decisions, such as what approach to adopt for a grammar item or structure, were influenced not only by their stated beliefs but also by the time they perceived they would have to complete an activity. Velma suggested after the study when she heard the results that she continued to employ the traditional approach to teaching grammar in her lessons because of these time factors and this despite her now stated preference for a communicative approach to teaching grammar. By way of summary, Richards *et al.* (1996) discovered the following beliefs that teachers in Hong Kong believed about their role in the classroom that may be a useful guide for other teachers to reflect and compare with their own beliefs:

- provide useful language learning experiences
- provide a model of correct language use
- answer learners' questions
- correct learners' errors
- help students discover effective approaches to learning
- pass on knowledge and skills to their students
- adapt teaching approaches to match students' needs.

Second language teachers are not the only players that hold beliefs about teaching and learning – students also hold beliefs about teaching and learning language; however, these beliefs may not be the same for both sets of players. Barnes (1976), for example, maintains that the language a teacher actually uses in his or her classroom performs two functions simultaneously: it carries the message that the teacher wants to communicate, while at the same time it conveys specific information: who the teacher is; whom he/she is talking to, and what the teacher believes the situation is; the teacher's frame of reference. So, the way a teacher organizes patterns of classroom communication depends on the teacher's frame of reference (beliefs) which is influenced by the teacher's prior experiences as a student, the teacher's theories about how a subject should be learned and/or the teacher's beliefs about how a subject should be taught. Barnes (1976: 18) has maintained that 'learning is not just a matter of sitting there waiting to be taught'. In this regard, Richards *et al.* (1991) noted that the kinds of learners teachers thought did best in their classes included those who:

- were motivated
- were active and spoke out
- were not afraid of making mistakes
- could work individually without the teacher's help.

Language teachers must thus be given opportunities to be able to articulate their beliefs and what they mean to them and if they still remain valid in light of present-day research in teaching and learning before being encouraged to make any changes. After articulating and reflecting on their beliefs about teaching and learning, language teachers should be encouraged to reflect on their actual classroom practices to see if there is alignment between their stated beliefs and their classroom practices. When comparing the teachers' stated beliefs with their actual classroom practices in the case study reported on in this chapter, for the most part both teachers showed a strong sense of convergence between their stated beliefs and actual classroom practices. For example, Daphne's classroom practices of providing explicit explanations and instructions on grammar items and structures were congruent with her belief in her 'traditional approach to grammar teaching'. Velma's belief in a more indirect, or covert, approach to grammar teaching partially matched some of her actual classroom practices. The case study presented in this chapter investigated the extent to which teachers' beliefs influenced their classroom practices, and found further evidence to suggest that what teachers say and do in the classroom is strongly governed by their tacitly held beliefs. The point in reflecting on the alignment between beliefs and classroom practices is not to suggest that one method of teaching is better than any other. Exploring language teachers' beliefs and corresponding classroom practices can help clarify how teachers can implement any changes to their approaches to teaching and learning over time. This type of reflection is possible through many of the activities that are covered in this book including reflecting on teachers' narratives (Chapter 2 and Chapter 4), classroom communication patterns (Chapter 7), teachers' language proficiency (Chapter 5), teachers' metaphors and maxims (Chapter 6), teaching journals (Chapter 9), group discussions (Chapter 10), classroom observations (Chapter 11) and concept maps (Chapter 13).

However, teachers must also realize that students also have beliefs and values and purposes for learning. In addition, students interpret (through their frame of reference) what teachers say by filtering the information through their preexisting beliefs, as this is the only way they can make sense of it. As Barnes (1976: 21) maintains, every student will 'go away with a version of the lesson which in some respects in different from all other pupils' versions, because what each student brings to the lesson will be different'. It is interesting to note that the two teachers reported on in the case study presented in this chapter were not consciously aware of their own beliefs about teaching and learning English language until directly asked by the interviewers. In addition, they were not consciously aware of their classroom practices concerning the teaching of grammar, and as such they had no way of comparing their beliefs and classroom practices. Also, they stated that they had not even considered asking their students to reveal their beliefs about grammar teaching and learning. The following excerpt from an ESL class on reading comprehension in Hong Kong shows how the lesson did not go according to the teacher's intended plan because the students had a different frame of reference. The teacher has just finished giving instructions to her students about their grammar homework and was answering questions about previous homework (Data Source: Tsui, 1995: 2–3).

1. S1: Do we need to draw a picture?
2. T: Draw what picture?
3. S1: The...
4. T: No, you don't have to draw the pictures, just write the sentences. All right, now will you take out your green book four.
5. S1: Mrs K, do we need to write number one on the book?
6. T: No, you don't have to write number one, otherwise it would be twelve pairs of sentences, wouldn't it? Eleven pairs.

7. S2: Do we get the green book four?
8. T: Green book four, yes. You know it's reading lesson, why don't you get it out ready? All right, now, green book four. Last week, we were reading Kee Knock Stan. What is Kee Knock Stan? Janice.
9. S3: I cannot understand
10. T: Yes, And what language is it supposed to be? Julia.
   (*cannot hear answer*)
11. T: Right. And where is Lalloon Land supposed to be?
12. Ss: Silence
13. T: Do you think there is a real country called Lalloon Land?
14. Ss: No.
15. T: T: No. But in the story, what does it say about Lalloon Land?
16. Ss: Silence
17. T: Have you been to Lalloon Land?
18. Ss: (shake heads)
19. S4: (raises hand)
20. T: Michele?
21. S4: Can we give in our grammar on um Wednesday?
22. T: Can you give in your grammar on um Wednesday? You have a lot of homework for tomorrow?
23. Ss: Yes, yes.
24. S5: We have our last exercise.
25. T: You have to do –
26. S5: Our last exercise.
27. T: Oh that's because you have been lazy and didn't do your work properly. Right?
28. Ss: No.
29. T: So, I'm sorry, you have to do it, otherwise I won't be able to finish marking your books to give you back before the holidays.
   Key: S1 = student 1, T = teacher

From turns 1–4, it is evident that the teacher was trying to get on with her main pedagogical objective – teach reading from a text. However, from turns 5–20, it is evident that the lesson did not progress as she had planned. In fact, it becomes clear that the teacher's frame of reference and the students' frames of reference were very different: The teacher wanted to get on with the lesson and start teaching the reading passage from the text, but the students were really worried about their previous homework assignment because they did not understand it. They were especially concerned about getting the correct instructions for homework and they were worried that they did not have enough time to finish the homework assessment. So, the teacher's plan had to wait until she addressed her students' anxieties about their homework. Thus students could be surveyed about their beliefs concerning learning and teaching by asking them such questions (adapted from Richards and Lockhart, 1994) as:

- What do you think about English (or the target language if it is different from English)?
- What do you think is the most difficult aspect of learning English (or the target language if different from English)?
- What are the best ways to learn a second language?
- What kind of learners do best in class when learning a second language?
- What kind of learning style do you have?
- How do you see your role in the classroom?
- How would you define effective teaching?
- What are the qualities of a good teacher?
- What do you think about the role of textbooks in your language course or programme?
- What do you think about the assessments used in this course or programme?
- What changes would you like to see in this course or programme?

In addition to answering the questions posed above for students, teachers can also ask themselves the following questions (adapted from Richards and Lockhart, 1994) about their beliefs and practices:

- What are my beliefs about teaching and learning?
- How do these beliefs influence my teaching?
- Where do my beliefs come from?
- What way do I actually teach in the classroom and how do I know?
- What do my learners believe about learning?
- What do my learners believe about my teaching?
- How do these beliefs influence their approach to learning?
- What learning strategies do my learners adopt?
- What learning styles do my learners favour?
- What is my role as a language teacher?

- How does this role contribute to my teaching style?
- What do my learners perceive as my role as teacher?

When teachers critically reflect on the answers they give to the above questions they can develop a deeper understanding of their beliefs and experiences and use this new understanding as a basis for making more informed decisions about their teaching. As Richards and Lockhart (1994: 6) maintain, reflecting on beliefs and practices 'involves posing questions about how and why things are the way they are, what value systems they represent, what alternatives might be available, and what the limitations are of doing things one way as opposed to another'. Consequently, they maintain if teachers are active reflectors of what is happening in their own classroom, they better position themselves to discover whether there is any gap between what they teach and what their students learn.

One final word concerning possible limitations of teachers articulating their beliefs if they do not also compare these stated beliefs with their classroom practices. That is, second language teachers may vary to the extent they can articulate their beliefs in that teachers may not be able to verbalize why they have made a particular decision partly because these beliefs are forever changing (Senior, 2006), and even when beliefs have been articulated, they may be an unreliable guide to the reality of their classroom actions (Pajares, 1992). As such, when beliefs have been stated, teachers should monitor their classroom practices to see if there is evidence of these beliefs in classroom practices (deductive approach), or alternatively, teachers can look at their teaching first and then stand back and examine what beliefs are being manifested through actual classroom practices (inductive approach). Senior (2006: 261) has pointed out the strong link between beliefs and practices when teachers in her study were faced with a position of having to teach in ways that conflicted with their teaching beliefs which resulted in one teacher subverting the system so that she could 'continue to teach in the way she believed was right'.

Reflection

➢ What are your beliefs about second language learning?
➢ What are your beliefs about second language teaching?
➢ Richards and Lockhart (1994: 3) have suggested that 'teachers are often unaware of what they do when they teach'. Do you agree or disagree with them? Why or why not?

➤ Do your classroom practices reflect your stated beliefs in both language learning and language teaching? How do you know?

➤ How would you go about investigating if your stated beliefs are congruent with your actual classroom practices?

➤ How have your past experiences as a language learner influenced you as a language teacher?

➤ How much are you influenced to continue to use activities that have worked well in your classes?

➤ Are you or have you even, been, influenced to continue to use established practices within a school?

➤ What would you do if a school wanted you to teach in a way that ran contrary to your beliefs?

➤ What would you do if you were asked to teach a textbook designated for a course that you are teaching that ran counter to your personal beliefs such as a book of grammar explanations for a speaking class?

➤ How much of your personality influences your teaching style?

➤ How has research in second language education influenced your teaching?

➤ Has your teaching been influenced by any one method or a combination of methods?

Conclusion

Language teachers need to be challenged to reflect on their existing beliefs and classroom teaching practices and to 'question those beliefs in the light of what they intellectually know and not simply what they intuitively feel' (Johnson 1999: 39). The purpose of examining language teacher beliefs and classroom practices is not to look at or for 'best practices'; rather, the idea is to see what *is* so teachers can become more confident knowing that what they believe about language teaching and learning is being practised in their classes. Since language teachers' beliefs about successful teaching form the core of their teaching behaviour, this chapter has suggested that opportunities be provided for practising language teachers to articulate and reflect on their beliefs and classroom practices while also investigating any discrepancies between their beliefs and classroom practices. As Woods (1996: 71) has cautioned, language teachers must be on guard against any claim of 'allegiance to beliefs consistent with what they perceive as the current teaching paradigm rather than consistent with their unmonitored beliefs and their behaviour in class'.

Chapter scenario

Frank, an EFL teacher, decided to reflect on his beliefs about communicative language teaching and especially teaching English conversation, by monitoring his classes over a period of five weeks using a teaching journal. After monitoring his classes in this way over the first four weeks he noticed a pattern developing in his journal entries which concerned his students' lack of response in his conversation class; he felt disappointed because his students were not responding well to the various activities he introduced during these classes. As this was an English conversation class, he had expected them to speak more than him during the class even though they were false beginner level students (they studied grammar rules in class, but did not practise using the language much during the classes). He had used activities that encouraged students to speak rather than read, listen or write because he believed this was the best approach to communicative language teaching. Frank reflected as follows in one entry in his teaching journal: 'I was trying to introduce the idea of learning strategies during this period of reflection but the class had not gone well. I interpreted the students' lack of response because they just returned from a long vacation. Now I realize that I must work harder on my introductions to each lesson to make sure they understand what I am trying to get them to do during each class. I am unsatisfied, even after four classes. I had wanted them to talk more. I was not happy too because Sergio especially was speaking a lot using his native language in class. A good lesson for me is when students are talking together; today and the past few lessons they were not talking at all'. He continued a few days later in his journal: 'From now on I am going to write all my instructions on the board in English and get one of the students to explain what I want them to do during that particular class. Then if they do not respond, at least I will know it has nothing to do with the instructions I give. I will use this process of elimination to see what is going wrong and what is going right in my class'.

Reflection

- What do you think of Frank's method of reflecting on his beliefs?
- Do you think he was successful with this method? Why or why not?

- Discuss other procedures of reflection that Frank could have used to reflect on his beliefs about communicative language teaching.
- Think about your first years of teaching and compare what you did then with what you do now.
- What are some of the important ways your approach to teaching has changed (e.g., my teaching is not as teacher-centred as before)?
- What are the sources of the changes you identified above?

Teachers' narrative 4

Introduction

In Chapter 2 teachers were encouraged to self-reflect by telling their life stories. This type of narrative reflection is important for language teachers because they can obtain new understandings of themselves as second language teachers when they reflect on their own perspectives of teaching and learning. However, Bell (2002) has suggested narrative inquiry goes beyond language teachers just simply telling stories and also features recounting specific classroom events and experiences. Narrative inquiry for language teachers as it is outlined in this chapter is grounded in Dewey's notion of reflecting on teachers' specific experiences, because a teacher's life is itself a narrative of the composite of these experiences such as specific critical incidents that happen both inside and outside the classroom as well as analysing specific case studies of teaching practices. Whereas Chapter 2 encouraged language teachers to look at the overall picture of their teaching lives, this chapter outlines how practising teachers can use narrative inquiry to analyse specific critical incidents, and case studies so that they can become more aware of what influences their practices.

What the research says

A critical incident is any unplanned and unanticipated event that occurs during class, outside class or during a teacher's career but is 'vividly remembered' (Brookfield, 1990: 84). Incidents only really become critical when they are subject to this conscious reflection, and when language teachers formally analyse these critical incidents, they can uncover new understandings of their practice (Richards and Farrell, 2005). An incident can appear to be typical rather than critical at first sight, and becomes critical through analysis by viewing it in terms of something that has significance in the wider context (Tripp, 1993). Thus, when a critical incident occurs, it interrupts (or highlights) the taken for granted ways of thinking about teaching, and by analysing such incidents teachers can examine the values and beliefs that underpin their perceptions about teaching.

Another means of engaging in teacher narratives is to reflect on case studies of specific events that occur in a teacher's work. Whereas a critical incident is a retrospective analysis of any unexpected incident, a case study starts with the identification of an issue and then the selection of a case-method procedure for reflecting on it. A case is a freeze-frame of a classroom situation that allows time for reflection (Schön, 1983). Case materials can be written and videotaped and provide a detailed means for helping teachers develop a capacity to explore and analyse different situations and dilemmas. Thus by reproducing and attempting to relive one specific situation, the case typifies the sort of dilemma that many teachers may face during their careers. They allow for a bridging of the gap between theory and practice. Shulman (1992: 2) maintains that cases can be used to teach:

1. principles or concepts of a theoretical nature,
2. precedents for practice,

3. morals or ethics,
4. strategies, dispositions and habits of mind, and
5. visions or images of the possible.

Case studies give raw information about what teachers actually experience from their frames of reference and are particularly helpful for other teachers to examine because of the insider viewpoint. Case reports can show how peers have dealt with similar teaching incidents, such as critical incidents discussed above and when deconstructed through a process of questioning and analysis, they can show how teachers' beliefs and knowledge form the basis for how they act in many situations. As Shulman (1992) maintains: 'Case-based teaching provides teachers with opportunities to analyze situations and make judgments in the messy world of practice, where principles often appear to conflict with one another and no simple solution is possible' (p. xiv). Research indicates then that when teachers analyse specific events and situations as outlined in critical incidents and case reports they can:

- gain a greater level of self-awareness
- learn how to identify important issues
- learn how to frame problems
- develop an awareness of teaching/learning complexities
- learn how to pose critical questions about teaching
- bring underlying beliefs to the level of awareness
- realize that there are no simple solutions or answers
- learn how to summarize common emotional experiences
- learn how to create opportunities for action research.

Case study I: ESL teacher's critical incident

The following critical incident was reported by an experienced second language teacher in Canada. The critical incident is reported in the teacher's own words and in four different sections as follows:

- *Orientation*: This part answers the following questions: Who? When? What? Where?
- *Complication*: Outlines what happened and the problem that occurred along with any turning point in the story.

- *Evaluation:* This part answers the question: So what? What this means for the participants in the story.
- *Result:* This part outlines and explains the resolution to the complication.

Orientation

I was teaching a course entitled Socio-cultural Influences on Teaching English as a Second Language. It was in the autumn term; three hours per week; most were university graduates who wanted to become ESL/EFL teachers. The survey is called the Key Performance Indicators (KPI) and it is done across the province by all colleges. It is the primary source of information about the course and we are held accountable for the responses. For example, in previous years, there was a very low part of our KPIs related to college facilities and we, as a department, had to hold a focus group with our students to better understand their responses. We discussed it with our program advisory committee, and the program chair had to come up with strategies for improvement. It asks students to comment on a very wide range of things from the actual learning experience and program quality to college resources, facilities, technology, cafeteria/bookstore, skills for future career, right down to teacher punctuality. They complete it at the end of the program. Not all courses in a program have to do it every term and not all programs necessarily do one every year. Because it is so extensive, they take a cross section of programs in the college. (I think). It is the type where a statement is given and the students can mark an answer their answer on a continuum: Agree strongly, agree, neither agree nor disagree, disagree, disagree strongly (something like that).

The student in this incident was one who had repeatedly, from the very first class demonstrated a contemptuous boredom with the program as a whole. He had indicated this in a number of ways to all his teachers. In person, he was tactfully polite, but in his written assignments, he would express his truer feelings. He always seemed to resist or think he was above what we were teaching in the program. We suspected that his fiancée, who was also in the program, had dragged him there so that they could travel overseas together. He had just completed university and seemed to think he was above a college program; although, this is now my own perception, as I seek to understand why someone would stay in a program that he clearly didn't like. Because the negative feedback came from this student, I could have dismissed it more easily . . . it was predictable; of course he didn't like anything. It was really not a surprise. And yet, I still felt the sting of the negative result and comments and had to reflect upon why.

Complication

When we did our official surveys and I could tell from, you know how they give you the bar graph or the percentages showing, you know disagreed, neutral, and then agree. Seven percent were always that disagree, which indicates out of a class of whatever it was, 19 or whatever that one person HATED everything.

Evaluation

I was very disturbed by some unsolicited comments from a TESL student at the end of December. Even after all our talk about feedback from students and our ability to take feedback and make changes, and not taking it personally. I was amazed by my hugely, negative, emotional response. Just when you think you're above the fray, bam some negative feedback hits you between the eyes. After doing some thinking on the experience, I have come to realize that it wasn't the comment itself that disturbed me (basically because I knew it was not valid), but the fact that this student felt he had a right to criticize the course content (and indirectly me) despite the fact that he had not attended a significant portion of the course and actually failed the final exam. The fact is that I felt vulnerable. I think I was worried that someone (other teachers???? Not sure) was going to listen to this guy and that judgments would be made about this course and about me.

Result

I'm totally over that. In fact, I think I am probably a more severe critic of myself than anyone else could be. I wasn't concerned by the positives or the negatives or the neutrals. I mean I looked at them and it was interesting and there were not really surprising things but I knew that that was him and it was like, oh well. So I feel empowered by our PD (professional development). I don't know if it's a direct result of our PD. The surveys never actually give you anything really, really concrete to do in your class but you get this feedback and then you're like, well what do I . . . What do I do with this? How does it affect me? Now, it's different. So, I think by openly discussing the surveys . . . Then today, today I had to send out the 'Have Your Say,' like our ESL teachers do a mid-term survey called Have Your Say. Basically the way it's structured is the different skills thumbs-up/thumbs-down.

Case study I reflection

➤ How did analysing the critical incident in Case Study I above lead the teacher above to a greater awareness of her practice?

➤ Now analyse the above incident with a colleague and see if you give a different interpretation or insight into the meaning of the story.

➤ Have you ever experienced a critical incident like the one above concerning fear of class surveys? If so, describe the incident and explain why it was critical to you.

Case study II: Should I give the rule or get on with the lesson?

The following incident was reported by an English language teacher in Singapore (Farrell, 2003). The class from High School that is discussed here is an English language class that is considered to have above average English language proficiency skills. The class consisted of 40 students, and the teacher prepared sentence examples on an overhead transparency before the class. When asked by the observer (after the class) what he thought the students had learned in the lesson, the teacher said he could not tell for sure. The teacher said that he was not sure how to teach subject–verb agreement as a grammar structure but only realized this when he started to answer the questions (on the overhead transparency) he had set for the students. Suddenly, he said that in the middle of the lesson he thought: 'Should I give the rule or get on with the lesson?'. He knew at that moment that he did not have a firm set of beliefs about the place of grammar in the curriculum. Thus, he was faced with the dilemma of whether to give the grammar rule to the class or continue with what he had planned for that lesson. Initially, he wanted to conduct an inductive grammar lesson. However, as the lesson progressed he became less focused because of many additional and contributing factors. For example, the teacher's lesson objectives were full of vague statements, and the lesson lacked concrete activities that would have enabled the students to interact more with each other. The teacher did not check the students' prior knowledge of subject–verb agreement before he started the lesson, nor did he know why he chose this particular grammar structure to teach. The teacher used grammar examples that he was not comfortable with, or did not know. In addition, during the class, the teacher's instructions throughout the lesson became less clear to the students.

The teacher said that his beliefs about the place of grammar (including his whole approach to teaching grammar) in English lessons was still unclear to him after the lesson and that he would have to rethink this.

Case study II reflection

➤ The statement made by the teacher above in Case Study II, 'Should I give the rule or get on with the lesson?', embodies the complexity of teaching English grammar in a real classroom situation. What do you think went through his mind immediately after this critical incident?

➤ How did analysing his classroom practices in Case Study II lead the teacher to a greater awareness of his beliefs?

➤ The teacher did not check the students' prior knowledge of subject–verb agreement before he started the lesson, nor did he know why he chose this particular grammar structure to teach. Why should he have checked for this knowledge before teaching the lesson?

➤ The teacher used grammar examples that he was not comfortable with, or did not really understand. What should he have done to prepare these before class?

➤ Have you ever experienced a critical incident like the one above concerning your teaching of grammar? If so, describe the incident and explain why it was critical to you.

From research to practice

Critical incidents

There are basically two main phases of reflecting on critical incidents: a description–production phase that is followed by an explanation phase (Tripp, 1993). In the description–production phase, some issue is observed and documented as an event or incident in which something happened. Thus the incident is 'produced'. The incident is then explained by the teacher in terms of its meaning, value or role to that particular teacher (Measor, 1985). Classroom critical incidents can be positive and/or negative events and may be identified by reflecting on a 'teaching high' or a 'teaching low' (Thiel, 1999). A teaching high in a language class could be a sudden change in the lesson plan teachers make during class because of their perceptions of the current events. They then decide to alter the events and this change in turn had some positive overall effect on the lesson such as more student response. A teaching low could be a specific classroom incident that was immediately problematic or puzzling for the teacher, such as one student suddenly crying during class for no apparent reason. Thiel (1999) suggests that by recalling and describing critical incidents like these one can begin to explore assumptions about effective teaching practice. The teacher in Case Study II did not have a firm set of beliefs about the place of grammar in the curriculum. The teacher said that he had not thought about this before class, and that he did not have a specific approach to teaching grammar. Thus, he was faced with the dilemma of whether to give the grammar rule or continue with what he was doing in the lesson. Initially, he wanted to conduct an inductive grammar lesson. It was not until he analysed this class critical incident that he realized his confusion of not only his teaching practices but also his beliefs. We can all learn from analysing this critical incident that teachers of English grammar (and other skill areas) should be aware of all the different approaches to teaching grammar, and that they should also be able to articulate their own personal beliefs about the place of grammar teaching in English language lessons. Critical incidents can also be general incidents that have occurred outside the classroom but have had an impact on the teacher and even resulted in a significant change in the teacher's personal as well as professional life. These can also be considered a turning point in a teacher's career and can be captured when the teacher examines episodes from his or her past. These career critical incidents can be represented in the form of an autobiographical sketch, or with the 'Tree of Life' as outlined in Chapter 2. Thiel (1999) suggests that the reporting of critical incidents (written or spoken) should follow specific steps:

- Self-observation – identify significant events that occur in the classroom.
- Detailed written description of what happened – the incident itself, what led up to it and what followed.
- Self-awareness – analyse why the incident happened.
- Self-evaluation – consider how the incident led to a change in understanding of teaching.

Case analysis

Whereas a critical incident involves looking back on an unplanned classroom incident and reflecting on its meaning, a case is broader and starts from identification of a particular issue and then involves selecting a method for collecting information about it. Of course identification of a critical incident can provide the initial motivation for a case study (Richards and Farrell, 2005). Preparing, reading and discussing cases provide information about teaching that is produced by teachers themselves that addresses their own real needs and issues. Teachers can write their own cases based on what actually happened in their classrooms or they can read and discuss cases prepared by other teachers such as can be found in such collections as the enormous TESOL Case Study series. As teachers discuss a case, they define problems, clarify issues, weigh alternatives and choose a course of action. These abilities compose critical reflection. Cases can also provide a focus for journal writing (see Chapter 9) and specific case examples can be a component of a teaching portfolio (see Chapter 2). Wassermann (1993) suggests that cases be processed by teachers in terms of three stages:

- *Fact-finding*: Before dealing with the situation or problem of a case, it is useful to generate questions about relevant facts and concepts. During this early stage, the emphasis is on surfacing all of the details that are possible clues for later analysis. This is one way for teachers who jump to premature solutions to slow down their thinking and to focus on the facts of the case only.
- *Meaning-making*: Now that you have completed the first stage of case analysis, you have accumulated a lot of information and need to make sense of it. One way of organizing the information from the point of view of making sense of it all is to use concept maps (see Chapter 12) to see the complex relationships that may have developed within a case. At this stage of case analysis, teachers attempt to identify the problems within the case from the teacher's view first and then their own points of view.
- *Problem-solving*: In the final stage of case analysis, teachers attempt to make decisions about the case based on the previous set of questions. The last two categories (meaning-making and problem-solving) are for the purposes of promoting teachers' growth in critical reflection.

The following are examples of case studies that could be used as part of a teacher reflection activity (from Richards and Farrell, 2005: 128–9).

- Information collected over a period of a semester concerning how two different students (one with high proficiency and one with low proficiency) performed during group activities.

- An account of the problems a teacher experienced during her first few months of teaching.
- An account of how two teachers implemented a team-teaching strategy and the difficulties they encountered.
- An account of observation of one high-achieving student and one low-achieving student over a semester in order to compare their patterns of classroom participation.
- A teacher's journal account of all of the classroom management problems she had to deal with in a typical school week.
- An account of how a teacher made use of lesson plans over a three-week period.
- An account of how two teachers resolved a misunderstanding that occurred between them in relation to the goals of a course.
- A description of all the changes a student made in a composition she was working on over a three-week period, from the drafting stage to the final stage.

Reflection

➢ When does an incident become critical for a language teacher during class?

➢ How can analysing critical incidents lead to a greater awareness of teaching?

➢ Have you ever experienced a critical incident during class? If so, describe the incident and explain why it was critical to you.

➢ Why is a case a 'freeze-frame' of a classroom situation?

➢ What is your understanding of the jazz maxim: 'You have to know the story in order to tell the story'?

➢ Suggest more examples of topics that would be suitable as the subject for teacher case reports.

➢ Look at the following incident and identify what makes it critical. Rachael, in her capacity as ESL teacher was sometimes asked to teach what were termed 'Remedial classes'. Rachael thought nothing of this labelling until one day she overheard one student ask another if he was a 'spastic' because he was in a remedial group. Rachael was appalled to hear this in her class.

➢ Write a short description of an incident from a recent teaching experience in terms of who, where, when and what happened. Next try to interpret where this incident fits into your beliefs, and theories of language teaching. Can you compare this incident with any other such incidents and/or events?

➢ The following may give you some ideas about where to search for career critical incidents:

- What experiences do you base your identity as a language teacher on?
- The most influential mentor for you through your early teaching career.
- Influential students you have encountered in your classes.

Conclusion

Narrative reflection as discussed in this chapter suggests that language teachers can choose from various different means of 'imposing order' (Johnson and Golombek, 2002: 4) on their seemingly disparate practices such as by analysing critical incidents and case studies. Both critical incident analysis and case analysis can stimulate the habit of reflective practice for language teachers. Indeed, by analysing critical incidents and case studies that 'conflicts with our expectations, we can come to a greater understanding of the expectations themselves – what our beliefs, philosophies, understandings, conceptions (of the classroom, of the language, of the students, of ourselves) actually are' (McCabe, 2002: 83). Analysing critical incidents and cases provides teachers with further opportunities to consolidate their theoretical understanding of their practices and can lead to further exploration of different aspects of teaching through later specific action research projects (see Chapter 8 for more details on how to set up action research projects).

Chapter scenario

Brian, a third year British English language teacher in the UK, has had a bit of trouble maintaining discipline and control in his classes this semester. He has tried to win the students over by being as friendly as possible to them both inside and outside class. He even brought them on class trips and paid for all himself. However, he noticed recently that two international students from the same country in one of his oral English classes whisper constantly together at the back of the room especially when he was teaching or trying to explain something. Brian sensed that the two students did not have much confidence in him as a teacher and suspected they were making fun of him but he was not sure because he did not understand their language. From time to time he asked them to stop talking to each other but they did not seem to pay much attention to him and soon began chattering away again in their mother tongue. Brian decided to establish a policy of giving students 20 per cent of their end of term grade based on their classroom participation and cooperation. Since he did not notice any change in the two disruptive students' behaviour at the end of the semester he only gave them 1 per cent for participation. When the two students received their grades they are very disappointed and asked to speak to Brian. In that meeting they explained to Brian that he was in fact their favourite teacher and that they really enjoyed his class and that is why they worked so hard to impress him, so they always decided to say a sentence in a whisper to each other to check it before saying it aloud in class. What Brian thought was chattering was actually the two students discussing or rehearsing the language they would need to use for a specific classroom activity. From this incident Brian realized that he should have spoken to the two students in private to find out why they were talking and to remind them what he was trying to achieve while teaching and when such talk could prove disruptive.

Reflection

- What made the incident above critical for Brian?
- How would you have reacted to what happened in Brian's class?
- Why do you think it is necessary for teachers to examine what went before and what comes after a particular critical incident?

Teachers' language proficiency **5**

Thomas S. C. Farrell and Jack C. Richards

Chapter Outline

Introduction

Most of the reflective activities discussed in this book are intended to assist language teachers with the development of their understanding of language teaching and of themselves as teachers. They are based on the assumption that teachers who engage in systematic reflection of their own teaching beliefs and practices will develop deeper insights, knowledge and strategies that will help them become better language teachers. But a fundamental component of a language teacher's professional competence is his or her proficiency in the language he or she teaches. The proficiency level of a language teacher will in many cases determine the extent to which the teacher is able to use many current teaching methods appropriately and whether the teacher is able to provide a reliable model of target language input for his or her students. Medgyes (2001) has maintained that 'the most important professional duty that non-native teachers have to perform is to make linguistic improvements in their English'. We could also add that it is also the duty of native speaker teachers to reflect on their knowledge and usage of English, especially if it is the language they are teaching. This chapter explores how teachers, especially non-native speaker teachers of English, can reflect on their language proficiency so that they can become more confident in teaching through the medium of English.

What the research says

Professional competence for most language teachers means acquiring a knowledge of relevant subject matter (e.g. learning theory, applied linguistics, pedagogical grammar, methodology), mastering a broad range of teaching skills, learning how to develop tests, curriculum and materials, how to use resources such as videos and computers, and especially for English language teachers who are not native speakers of the language they teach, proficiency in English. As Lafayette (1993:135) has suggested: 'Among the components of content knowledge, none is more important to foreign language teaching than language proficiency'. Language proficiency is defined in this chapter as 'knowledge, competence, or ability in the use of a language, irrespective of how, where, or under what conditions it has been acquired' (Bachman, 1990: 16) and is discussed in its own terms and does not consider whether the teacher has had any professional training.

Foreign language teachers who possess low language proficiency levels encounter problems when teaching in the language classroom because, as Berry has indicated (1990: 99), 'certain approaches to language teaching are incompatible with low levels of proficiency in teachers'. Medgyes (2001: 416) further points out that non-native speaker teachers because they may be preoccupied with their own language difficulties, are 'reluctant to loosen their grip over the class as group work and pair work often create unpredictable situations full of linguistic traps'. This is especially true for oral-based methodologies that many international language courses are based on, and especially true for English as a second/foreign language courses. For example, the ever popular communicative language teaching (CLT) approach to language teaching requires a relatively high level of proficiency on the part of the teacher and this in turn has made CLT difficult to implement in some parts of the world. However, research indicates that language teachers can use more of the language they are teaching while they are in class and thus develop more confidence when teaching (Richards, 1990). Richards (1990) outlined an example of detailed a case study of a teacher who wanted to increase the amount of English he was using in the classroom. The teacher checked tapes of three lessons he had audio-recorded at different times over a two-week period and first listened to them to determine the proportion of English to Japanese he was using and discovered that it was about 70 per cent English and 30 per cent Japanese. He then listened to the tapes again to find out the purposes for which he was using Japanese and found it was for two main purposes: classroom management and giving feedback. Later he drew up a plan to reduce the amount of Japanese he was using for these two purposes. He first consulted a guide to the use of English in the classroom (Willis 1981) and familiarized himself with English expressions that could be used for classroom management and feedback. He wrote out a set of expressions and strategies on cards and put these in a conspicuous place on his table. These served not only to remind him of his plan but also helped him remember some of the expressions he wanted to use. Each day he would place a different card on top of the pile. He then continued recording his lessons and after a few weeks checked his tapes and discovered that his use of Japanese had declined considerably.

Britten (1985) has noted that language improvement is probably the commonest need in in-service training for language teachers. Berry (1990: 98) speculates that such teachers probably do not have access to the target-language culture and native speakers, 'either at home or via foreign travel (which means teachers in the majority of the world)'. Research has also indicated that such perceptions are common among language teachers in many countries where English is a foreign language (EFL) (Maley, 1986). Such limited language proficiency is likely to influence the extent to which the teacher can manage the following aspects of teaching:

- provide good language models
- provide a sufficiently rich language learning input
- recognize errors in learners' production
- give appropriate feedback on learners' errors
- monitor his or her own speech and writing for accuracy
- teach a lesson in English without resorting to the mother tongue
- improvise within a lesson
- go beyond the textbook and add to or supplement the book
- use and adapt authentic materials
- provide language examples

- give accurate explanations (e.g. of vocabulary and language points)
- use appropriate classroom language
- access target-language resources (e.g. newspapers, magazines, internet)

Improving the language proficiency of teachers has obvious benefits for both the institution as well as teachers themselves who need such support such as:

- Higher standards of use of the target language for the institution and its teachers.
- Higher levels of learning within the institution.
- Access to higher levels of professional development for the teacher and institution.
- Improved skills for lesson planning and materials development.
- Personal satisfaction.
- Wider range of teaching methods available for the teacher, the institution and the students.

Case study: language awareness workshop

Johnson (1990) describes a workshop on classroom language within a basic professional training programme for Hong Kong Chinese secondary teachers in all subject areas. The programme sought not only to raise the awareness of the role language plays in the classroom, but also encouraged teachers to apply what they learned to their various subject areas. The course involved tasks that engaged teachers in exploring the nature and effectiveness of their classroom language. Each task or exercise had three stages: *Development*: particular teaching acts are identified and communication tasks are prepared which depend crucially for their success on the effective performance of those teaching acts. *Practice*: Teachers complete the communication tasks and evaluate their performances. *Application*: Teachers identify general principles governing the effective completion of such tasks and discuss ways of applying those principles to their own teaching subjects.

Of the 15 contact hours in the course, six were spent in the language laboratory, with students engaged in various tasks. The remaining hours were used for discussing issues raised by these tasks. The work in the language laboratory was divided into *individualized work, classwork,* and *pair work.* For individual-ized work, students controlled their own learning through activities in which they could record, replay and/or repeat target forms and utterances as often as they wanted such as prepare a set of instructions, or follow and evaluate the instructions prepared by another teacher. Pair work activities included role-play, simulation exercises, problem solving, communication gap exercises and discussion periods.

The workshop sessions examined various aspects of classroom language under three major headings: *physiological* aspects, *interpersonal* aspects and *pedagogical* aspects. The physiological aspect of classroom language dealt with the teacher's voice and voice projection. The interpersonal aspect of classroom language dealt with how teachers use language to control, organize and motivate learning. For example, language used to control and organize could be the teacher saying: 'Stand up!' and 'Move into your groups'. Motivational language could be the teacher praising the students as follows: 'Great, you are correct', and 'Good idea'. The pedagogical aspect of classroom language involved teachers using language in order to positively influence learning, such as giving clear instructions.

Case study reflection

➤ How do you think a teacher's language proficiency influences his or her teaching style?

➤ Willis (1981) suggests that non native-speaker teachers can combine a language improvement course and a methodology course. How can this be achieved?

➤ What would you like to see covered in language awareness workshops that focus on the following aspects of teacher-language or classroom language use (rank them in the order you would like to see them):

   ○ *common pronunciation problems of teachers of English*
   ○ *effective questioning techniques*
   ○ *strategies for presenting vocabulary in English*
   ○ *effective classroom language*
   ○ *the language of giving instructions*
   ○ *presenting dialogues*
   ○ *effective error correction*
   ○ *voice projection, intonation and voice tone*

From research to practice

General goals for language improvement opportunities for language teachers include the following:

- to improve teachers' proficiency in reading, writing, speaking and listening
- to develop their confidence in using English
- to further develop their knowledge about English
- to improve their capacity for self-assessment of their language use
- to develop an awareness of the nature of classroom discourse
- to develop strategies for carrying out common classroom functions in English
- to develop less of a dependence on the textbook as a primary teaching resource

A number of sources of information can be used to identify the needs for language so that they can pursue these goals. For example, language teachers can be surveyed either formally or informally to find out what kinds of language needs they feel they have. Teachers can personalize their language learning objectives by designing a study plan that takes their personal needs and learning style into consideration. Language improvement can also be the focus of peer coaching (see Chapter 12). Identifying a teacher's limitations in the area of classroom language use can be a task assigned to a peer coach if that coach has exhibited superior language proficiency skills. The coach and the teacher then identify strategies for language improvement. For example, the teacher may have asked the peer (as coach) to visit his or her class because he or she was not confident or comfortable about conducting pair work and group work in English. During a series of classroom observations the peer coach then observes and documents how the teacher sets up pair work and group work and notes the type of language the teacher uses as well as other relevant aspects of the teacher's language such as voice projection. After observing a series of lessons the teacher and coach discuss the findings and any problems that were observed. If necessary, the coach (with suggestions from the peer) can draw up examples of appropriate language that the teacher could use in the future when setting up pair work or group work. Examples of such types of language could be: 'In your pairs (groups) I'd like you to discuss . . . ' 'When you have finished, change groups so that you can take the other part'. The coach and the teacher can later monitor the teacher's efforts to use such language in carrying out pair and group work.

Language proficiency or classroom language use can also be the focus of a language teacher development group (see Chapter 10). For example, a group of teachers may be interested in improving their use of vocabulary in the classroom. As with peer coaching, they could start by watching videos of their own classrooms and focus on how they introduced and taught vocabulary. They could also watch videos of other teachers (including native-speaker teachers if available) teaching vocabulary or dealing with vocabulary problems in other classes. They can then compare and discuss their findings as a group. Also, the group can read articles from teaching magazines or reference books on teaching vocabulary in order to facilitate their discussions. As a group, they can then discuss and practise appropriate language to use when teaching vocabulary such as: 'First I want to make sure you know/understand the meaning of the word...' 'Does anyone know the meaning of...' 'Can anyone guess the meaning of...', 'I'll give you a clue. It has something to do with...'

A group of language teachers can also use resources available in the outside community. For example, activities can be arranged for non-native speaker teachers to view a recent movie in English, perhaps followed by a discussion activity. Similarly they can watch and discuss television programmes or videos in English and then share their reactions to them. Teachers can also be encouraged to borrow newspapers, books, video-tapes, audio-tapes, CD-ROMs and other materials from a library or download articles from the internet. Discussion groups can be set up to design follow-up activities. Individual teachers or groups of teachers can keep a record of their reading materials to better facilitate group discussions later. Teachers can discuss what they read (watched, listened to), what they thought about it, what they learned (if anything) and if they would recommend others to read (watch, listen to) the same material.

Sometimes in-service courses can be provided that combine methodology with language development. Roberts (1998) describes one such community-provided programme for the professional development of primary-school teachers of English in Spain that had a combined objective of developing English-language skills and knowledge of methodology. The teachers volunteered for the course after which they could obtain a higher degree, which is recognized throughout Spain. The contents of the programme included language improvement activities, activities to stimulate development in the teachers' personal theories of teaching and learning, methodology and language study, issues in and practice of classroom data collection techniques related to teaching plans, and classroom enquiry and personal supervision. The language proficiency objectives of the course were as follows:

- Develop teachers' awareness of English as a system.
- Develop teachers' general and course-specific language skills.
- Develop teachers' linguistic confidence and their ability to use English for professional purposes.

Objectives were also developed for the methodology component. This course served as a means of combining a language improvement component and a methodology component, or as Berry (1990) suggested: 'killing two birds with one stone'.

Clearly one does not need to be a native speaker of a language to teach it as a foreign or second language (despite the fact that this is sometimes the only qualification required of many people hired to teach in private language schools in many parts of the world). But how well does one need to speak a language in order to be able to teach it effectively? Commenting on the situation with regards to foreign language teachers in the United States, Layfette (1993:135) posits: 'Each of the four national associations that have issued statements on the level of proficiency needed for teaching have done so using the ACTFL Proficiency Guidelines. In all cases the recommended minimum level of proficiency is either Advanced or High Advanced'.

The language proficiency of a non-native language teacher working in a non-English speaking environment is likely to be influenced by a number of factors specific to the nature of language teaching. Since the teacher is typically teaching students of limited language proficiency the teacher's own classroom language is likely to be intentionally simplified in order to facilitate comprehension. Language teachers hence typically speak at a slower than normal speech rate, attempt to use simple vocabulary that is familiar to learners and avoid complex syntax and unfamiliar idioms. Their classroom discourse may have the following characteristics: It focuses on the formation of correct examples of language. It is in a careful (monitored) speech style. It involves use of small samples of language. It involves restricted types of communication.

While the teacher's strategy of providing learners with comprehensible input is desirable from the learners' point of view, it can also promote a type of fossilization in the teacher's own language. Language teachers in English as a Foreign Language (EFL) countries for example, may find that the only occasions they have to use English are with students in their own classrooms, since staffroom discussions and teachers' meetings may be conducted in the mother tongue. They are deprived of opportunities to develop their language proficiency. Over time due to the restricted type of English they use in the classroom and their restricted opportunities to use or hear 'normal English', their own English fails to develop. So, in order for the teacher's language to improve, opportunities are need for what Swain (1999) calls 'pushed output' that require the teacher to reshape his or her language and to use more complex structures and a wider range of vocabulary. Without opportunities to stretch their output they will tend to keep using a restricted lexicon and syntax and show little improvement or development over time, since the restricted purposes for which they use English do not push them to expand or restructure their linguistic resources. Language teachers need to have reached a certain threshold level of proficiency in the language in order to be able to teach effectively in it. Lack of proficiency often leads to excessive use of the mother tongue rather than English (or the foreign language) with practice of the language limited to exercises from the textbook. As Layfayette (1993: 128) comments, when the teacher has a poor command of the language he or she is teaching, the language

> becomes a subject that exists between the covers of a textbook, with the teacher's objective being the completion of so many lessons in an academic year or semester. Unfortunately, these values are often transferred to the students, who also eventually view the learning of as foreign language as the completion of textbook activities rather than the ability to use the language for purposes of communication. On the other hand, the proficient teacher, who has command of the subject matter and who uses the target language as the vehicle of instruction, is an obvious reminder to the students of the power of learning another language.

Reflection

➤ List some of the ways you think can be used to help teachers improve their language proficiency.

➤ How do you think the teacher's language proficiency influences his or her teaching style?

➤ Discuss how limited language proficiency can influence the extent to which the teacher can manage the following aspects of teaching:
  o provide good language models
  o provide a sufficiently rich language learning input

- ○ recognize errors in learners' production
- ○ give appropriate feedback on learners' errors
- ○ monitor his or her own speech and writing for accuracy
- ○ teach a lesson in English without resorting to the mother tongue
- ○ provide language examples
- ○ use appropriate classroom language

➤ How do you think the teacher's language proficiency influences his or her teaching style?

➤ Medgyes' (2001) research indicates that non-native speaker teachers of English tend to focus their teaching attention on accuracy and especially on mastery of grammar rules and that they prefer to rely on a textbook. What do you think of these research results?

➤ In some countries, native-speaker teachers are given different kinds of teaching assignments from non-native teachers. What are your views of this policy?

➤ This chapter gives several examples of indirect approaches to facilitate language improvement (e.g. workshops, reading groups, self-access activities). How can these and other activities be used to help in improving language proficiency?

Conclusion

Since many language teachers are non-native speakers of the language they speak, they need to not only attain but also maintain a certain acceptable level of proficiency in the language so that they are able to teach it effectively. Heaton (1981) has maintained that the language used in the classroom by language teachers contains a specific set of speech acts and functions and language teachers need to have attained fluency in these to be able to give instructions and directions clearly in English while teaching. As Heaton (1981: 14) maintains: 'Language cannot be divorced from content and practice' and that by improving language skills, a teacher can 'improve the particular teaching skills which involve the use of those skills'.

Chapter scenario

A group of three non-native English speaking EFL teachers in Turkey, Axiel, Subeda and Fazel, came together as a group to develop their English language proficiency levels. Each teacher had not been able to reflect on their particular use of English while they were teaching and wondered if they were using correct English in classroom situations. They first decided to read up on appropriate classroom language and discovered Heaton's (1981) specific examples of classroom discourse that include speech acts and functions such as:

- *requesting, ordering and giving rules*
- *establishing attention*
- *questioning*
- *repeating and reporting what has been said*
- *giving instructions*
- *giving and refusing permission*
- *warning and giving advice*
- *giving reasons and explaining*

They also read about Willis' (1981: 1) ideas of classroom language and her observations that teachers check their language use during the lesson as follows:

- *getting organized: seating, books, blackboard*
- *checking attendance*
- *the beginning of the lesson*
- *introducing different stages of the lesson*
- *dividing the class up: choral, individual and teams*
- *interruptions: late comers, things lost*
- *control and discipline*
- *ending the lesson or a stage in the lesson*

So the group decided to observe each other teaching and reflect on their use of language outlined above. They used this first observation to work out such issues as where the peer observers should sit (they decided at each corner in the back of the room), if they should write during the observations (they decided yes), and if they should interact with the students during the class (they decided not to). After this first observation all three felt less threatened by the peer observation process. The group then decided that each peer would write down the exact type of language the teacher used during the different stages of the lesson and compare notes after the observation. Later they realized that this would be too much work for each observer so they decided to break up the observation process. For example, Axiel decided to look at all the instructions she gives during class and the type of language she used while giving these instructions. Subeda decided to examine her use of group work during her oral English classes and the type of language she used to set up and monitor groups. Fazel decided to investigate how (the methods and results) she started and ended each class and the type of language she used to do this. They did this for two rounds of observations and then they met as a group to share their observations and discuss what they would do as a result of the findings. This latter meeting lasted for three hours and only accomplished each teacher giving an account of the classroom observations. They realized that they would have to have another meeting to evaluate and interpret these findings, and that after each teacher had a chance to digest what their peers had said. This next meeting produced interpretations by each group member and each teacher decided to make certain changes as a result of the meeting discussions.

Reflections

- What is your opinion of the way this group of teachers set up the observation process with the group?
- Try to add other suggestions for this group observation process.
- If you were going to have two other peer teachers observe you teach, how would you organize this process?
- What would you want to learn about your teaching from having two teachers observe you teach?
- Try to add more items to the checklist.

Teachers' metaphors and maxims 6

Introduction

Practising language teachers have accumulated images about learning and teaching that influence what they do in their classrooms. According to Senge (1990: 175) metaphors, or mental models, are what humans carry in their heads 'in the form of images, assumptions and stories... and not only determine how we make sense of the world, but how we take action'. However, many teachers may not be aware of the impact of these images on their current teaching practices, because they are held tacitly. So at some time during their careers teachers should explore the images, metaphors and maxims they have built up; as Burns (1999: 147) maintains, the metaphors that teachers hold can be used as 'an introspective and reflective tool'. This chapter outlines and describes how second language teachers can explore and reflect on their use of metaphors and maxims in order to become more aware of the impact of these on their classroom practices.

What the research says

A metaphor, defined by Dickmeyer (1989: 151) as 'the characterisation of a phenomenon in familiar terms', is often used by people to simplify their experiences. Lakoff and Johnson (1980: 232–3) suggest that a large part of self-understanding is the 'search for appropriate personal metaphors that make sense of our lives . . . The process of self-understanding is the continual development of new life stories for yourself'. Metaphors are also an important part of teachers' personal practical knowledge that shapes their understanding of their role as teachers. Pajak (1986: 123), for example, maintains that metaphors can be a means for teachers to verbalize their 'professional identity'. Metaphors are indications of the way teachers think about teaching and also guide the way they act in the classroom and thus when teachers begin to unpack the meaning of the metaphors they hold, they can begin to understand what they really believe about teaching and can start to transform themselves as teachers (Clandinin, 1986).

In early research that reviewed the metaphors that second language teachers use, Block (1992: 44) discovered both 'macro' and 'micro' metaphors and the two most common of the macro-metaphors used by teachers to describe their roles as: teacher as contracted professional who coordinates but not dominates their students' classroom activities, and teacher as a providing parent who encourages his/her students. For learners, Block (1992) identified two further macro-metaphors as: learner as respected client and learner as respected child. Block (1992) later discovered the following metaphors used in addition to the two macro-metaphors above – teacher as: researcher, God, devoted professional, comrade/friend and enforcer. Recently one of the most comprehensive literature reviews on the study of metaphor usage in second language teaching was conducted by Oxford *et al.* (1998). Oxford *et al.*'s (1998) typology covers four perspectives of teaching second language:

1. *Social order*: e.g., teacher as manufacturer; teacher as competitor.
2. *Cultural transmission*: e.g., teacher as conduit, teacher as repeater.
3. *Learner-centred growth*: e.g., teacher as nurturer; teacher as lover; teacher as scaffolder; teacher as entertainer.
4. *Social reform*: e.g., teacher as acceptor; teacher as learning partner.

Research has uncovered the following metaphors that second language teachers use

- *teacher as manufacturer*
- *teacher as competitor*
- *teacher as nurturer*
- *teacher as lover*
- *teacher as scaffolder*
- *teacher as entertainer*
- *teacher as learning partner*

In addition to the exploration and reflection on metaphors used, teachers can also explore the maxims, or dictums, they use to explain specific classroom actions. This is an important addition to the reflection on teacher images because as Richards (1996: 286) notes, a teacher's maxims 'function like rules for best behaviour' and also guide a teacher's classroom actions just like metaphors. Richards (1996) maintains that exploring teachers' maxims is an attempt to understand language teaching in its own light because it reveals the working principles which teachers adhere to as they teach. For example, Tsui (1995: 357) explored the personal maxims of two ESL teachers in the same Hong Kong secondary school and discovered two very different approaches to teaching the same subject, the same class and the same level. One teacher, a Chinese female, was a strict disciplinarian and followed a *maxim of order* which was based on her cultural and educational background which 'valued subservience to authority and emphasized observation to protocol'. The other teacher, a native of New Zealand, encouraged a more informal relationship with his students and his classes were very different from those of the first teacher because of his Western cultural background in which Tsui (1995: 359) points out, 'more emphasis was placed on the individual, most classrooms had done away with the traditional protocol, and the relationship between students and teachers was much less formal'. Research has also uncovered the following maxims language teachers use:

- The maxim of accuracy: work for accurate student output.
- The maxim of efficiency: make the most efficient use of class time.
- The maxim of empowerment: give the learners control.
- The maxim of encouragement: seek ways to encourage student learning.
- The maxim of planning: plan your teaching and try to follow your plan.
- The maxim of involvement: follow the learners' interests to maintain student involvement.

Case study: 'Teach the same way as I have been taught'

The following case study details the maxims a second language teacher used to guide her teaching in Singapore together with a classroom observer (Farrell, 2007). The case study highlights three main maxims the teacher used after her first classroom observation and how reflecting on these maxims contributed to positive changes in her teaching practices to promote more effective learning opportunities for her students.

- Maxim of apprenticeship of observation: *Teach the same way as I have been taught*

The first maxim that the teacher used was the maxim of apprenticeship of observation: 'teach the same way as I have been taught'. This is because the teacher said that she had decided to teach her classes in the same way as her teachers had taught her when she was a student. For example, for her second lesson observation the teacher decided to strictly follow the book and use worksheets because she said her secondary schoolteachers used this approach.

- Maxim of planning: *Finish the lesson at all costs*

The second maxim she used was the maxim of planning: 'finish the lesson at all costs'. She related that this maxim was her explanation of why all her lessons were carried out according to her original lesson plan regardless of what transpired during the lesson.

- Maxim of conformity: *Give observers what they want*

The third maxim presented here is the teacher's use of the maxim of conformity: 'give the observers what they want'. This maxim can be also linked to the chapter on classroom observations (see Chapter 11) and is important as many experienced language teachers have been observed while teaching for evaluation purposes and if the evaluator/observer was armed with a checklist, you may have been tempted to try to 'cover' as many items on the checklist as possible so the evaluator could check them off.

Case study reflection

➢ Have you ever used a maxim similar to the ones above indicating your teaching practices may be influenced by your past experiences as a student? Explain.

➢ Do you use any other maxim to explain what influences your practices? Explain.

➢ Have you ever used a maxim similar to the one above indicating your teaching practices may be overinfluenced by the presence of an observer in your class? Explain.

➢ Have you ever used a maxim similar to the one above indicating your teaching practices may be overinfluenced by your lesson plan? Explain.

➢ Do you use any other maxim to explain how you plan and execute lessons? Explain.

From research to practice

Metaphors

When language teachers reflect on their use of metaphors and maxims, they can examine who they really are as teachers and what guides them as they teach. When I was teaching recently in Singapore (Farrell, 2006b) I asked some teachers to answer the following questions: 'What is the teacher's role in the classroom? How should learning take place?'. Additionally, they were asked to complete the statement: 'A teacher is_____'. One teacher said that her perceptions of teaching were shaped by the following metaphor she used: *A classroom is a battleground.* She said that the classroom was a place of tension between the teacher and the student with both waiting to do battle. She continued: 'It is a battle between the students and the teacher. In the beginning, both parties do not know a lot about each other. The teacher has to fight to make the students receptive towards him/her'. For her the meaning of the word battle included an internal struggle for both teachers and students to use appropriate strategies within the classroom. The teacher remarked:

> There is a constant battle of making the right choices. The teacher has to decide what materials are suitable for the students. The students, on the other hand, have to choose among the choices and come up with a correct answer. In a battlefield the general has to decide what strategies to use to

defeat the enemies. Similarly, the teacher has to think of ways to finish the syllabus in time and also to make it interesting and captivating.

She also used the metaphors of the *teacher as a mother, teacher as a motivator* and *teacher as a facilitator,* and mentioned that all three metaphors were connected for her. She maintained that in order to motivate the students to learn English, the teacher has to facilitate the process by being a mother type to the students. She linked her use of *teacher as motivator* to her time as a student in the school system in Singapore when she noticed these qualities in her English language teacher. She explained as follows:

> As a motivator, I want to interest my students about the wonders of English language. I want them to enjoy English lessons (like I did) and not hate them. My English teachers have made my lessons interesting by teaching them with such zest. I will strive to be like them. When the students are motivated and interested, they would want to learn more about English. This will help them master the language even faster.

She clarified the *teacher as a mother* metaphor as the umbrella metaphor for her as a teacher. She says: 'I see myself as a mother to all my students. I do not want to be just their English teacher. I want to be a listening ear, a friend and someone they can turn to when they are in trouble'.

Consequently teachers can be asked to do the following:

- Finish this statement: 'An English language teacher is_____.'
- Finish this statement: 'A language student is_____.'
- Finish these statements:
    - 'A good second language teacher is_____.'
    - 'A good second language student is_____.'

As Berliner (1990: 86) has noted, for teachers, 'Metaphors are powerful forces, conditioning the way we come to think about ourselves and others'. Therefore, it is important for language teachers to be able to access these metaphors and to test their validity in light of current practices.

Maxims

In the case study reported in this chapter, the teacher was asked to identify the maxims she used to describe her teaching. When she identified and then reflected on the maxims she used to guide her teaching, she began to uncover her unconscious assumptions about teaching and learning. As she articulated and reflected on her maxims, she also began to realize that many of them may have been somewhat misguided and as a result may also have lead to self-defeating teaching behaviours in her classroom. For example, after reflecting deeply on her first maxim of apprenticeship of observation and its implications over a period of time, she began to see how her instructional decisions may have been overinfluenced by her past experiences as a student herself and thus she was imitating her own teachers' practices without much thought or reflection. When she realized this and decided that she no longer wanted to follow such practices, she began to formulate a new maxim similar to what Richards (1996: 290) has termed 'the maxim of encouragement: seek ways to encourage student learning' as she attempted to provide more learning opportunities for her students. Similarly, after much reflection and discussion on her maxim of planning, the teacher realized how the execution of her lessons was too heavily controlled by her lesson plan and not reactive enough to what actually transpired during the actual lesson. As Richards (1996) has noted, this is a situation where teachers see their students only as instruments in implementing and completing their lesson plan called the maxim of planning: 'plan your teaching and try to follow your plan' (Richards, 1996: 288). This approach, however, has a tendency to downplay students' interpretations and reactions to the lesson material and as such can block opportunities for learning. As the teacher reflected on this more, she began to articulate a different maxim to describe her instructional approach, one similar to what Richards (1996: 287) has termed 'the maxim of involvement: follow the learners' interests to maintain student involvement'. The teacher's use of this maxim of conformity, her third maxim can be partly explained by Richards (1996: 291) as follows: 'make sure your teaching follows the prescribed method'. In this case the 'prescribed method' was the teacher's attempt to predict what her observer wanted to see in her classes for evaluative purposes rather than teach the classes the way she 'would normally have done'. When she realized that she was 'under the spell of the observers' she began to move towards using a more appropriate maxim related to what she wanted her students to achieve and get from all her classes regardless of who was observing or not, and again she used the maxim of encouragement: 'seek ways to encourage student learning'. She said that in the future regardless of who was observing her teaching or for what reason, she would follow this new maxim. In such a manner second language teachers can be encouraged to reveal the maxims they would use to describe their practices and again test their validity in light of current practices.

Changing metaphors and maxims

When language teachers identify the metaphors and maxims they use, they can also be challenged as to their current relevance and then they can begin to develop alternative and more appropriate metaphors and maxims that best represent their practice. Language teachers may thus be able to restructure previously entrenched beliefs as they become more aware of the metaphors and maxims they use, and, as such, it may also be possible to trigger a repackaging of the old beliefs they held. So, by a process of critical reflection on metaphors and maxims (old and new), language teachers can understand and combine the unknown into what they already know (Provenzo *et al.*, 1989) as changes in metaphor and maxim usage signal changes in their conceptions of teaching and learning a second language. The real test of the teachers' metaphor and maxim usage is not whether they are 'right or wrong' according to an outsider's perceptions, but the extent to which they are useful for the teacher (Roberts, 1998). This is the key point in this chapter with regards to reflective teaching and professional development in that it is the practising teachers who decide whether to hold onto their present metaphors and maxims or to develop new ones that may better represent their current teaching state. As was pointed out in the case study reported on in this chapter, when the teacher realized that the maxims she had used to describe her work were not useful anymore, *she* came up with 'new' maxims as a result of her critical reflections on her practices.

Reflection

➤ What metaphor or maxim do you use for your role as a teacher?
➤ Has your use of this metaphor or maxim changed over time since you became a language teacher?
  o If yes, what differences have you noticed?
  o What experiences have led to the change you noticed?
  o If no changes have occurred in your metaphor usage, what experiences have resulted in this confirmation of your original metaphor usage?
➤ What metaphor or maxim do you use for the role of your students in your classes?
➤ Has your use of this metaphor or maxim changed over time since you became a language teacher?
  o If yes, what differences have you noticed?
  o What experiences have led to the change you noticed?

- o If no changes have occurred in your metaphor usage, what experiences have resulted in this confirmation of your original metaphor usage?
- ➤ What metaphor or maxim do you use for your perception of the role of classroom management styles for second language teachers?
- ➤ Has your use of this metaphor or maxim changed over time since you became a language teacher?
  - o If yes, what differences have you noticed?
  - o What experiences have led to the change you noticed?
  - o If no changes have occurred in your metaphor usage, what experiences have resulted in this confirmation of your original metaphor usage?
- ➤ In second language education, Block (1992) documented metaphors of both second language teachers and also their learners' use of metaphors that describe the teachers. Examine and discuss each of these and try to give examples that could be used from each one.
  - o Teachers' metaphors:
    - *teacher as a contracted professional*
    - *teacher as a providing parent*
  - o Learners' metaphors:
    - *teacher as detector of mistakes*
    - *teacher as seeker of effective methods*
    - *teacher as friend*
- ➤ Finish the sentences below concerning how you see teaching (from Bowen and Marks, 1994: 41):
  - o I see myself as an actor because_____
  - o I see myself as a guide because_____
  - o I see myself as a diplomat because_____
  - o I see myself as a waiter because_____
  - o I see myself as a chat-show host because_____
  - o I see myself as a coach because_____
  - o I see myself as a _____ because_____

Conclusion

When experienced second language teachers attempt to unpack and reflect on their use of metaphors, they can begin to probe their meaning in a relatively safe way, and if they discover any metaphors that may not be suitable for their teaching lives anymore, they can revise their metaphors in light of their present needs for teaching second language, for their students' learning that second language, for subject matter decisions and for their classroom environments. As such, a close examination of these metaphors may not only provide them with some insight into their prior beliefs, but also provide language teacher-educators with the same awareness which in turn can be an important starting point to initiate change in such metaphors if they conflict with what they see in their present surroundings.

Chapter scenario

Three teachers came together as a group in Singapore to reflect on their use and meaning of metaphors for their practice. They decided to try to answer (using metaphors) and discuss the following main questions in their group: 'What is the teacher's role in the classroom? How should learning take place?' Some of the metaphors they articulated included: *teacher as imparter of knowledge*; *teacher as moulder*; *teacher as mother*, *teacher as octopus*. One teacher explained the *teacher as imparter of knowledge* as follows: 'A teacher should impart skills in acquiring knowledge . . . a mandatory transfer of knowledge for the exams'. Another teacher said that the teacher must 'impart knowledge to facilitate learning. To build up each student's potential and to inculcate good character building'. The metaphor *teacher as moulder* was explained by a teacher as follows: 'A teacher should mould the students' characters by imparting values'. Additionally, the metaphor *teacher as octopus* was explained by a teacher to represent the many jobs, skills and responsibilities a teacher had to have in Singapore. The *teacher as mother* metaphor was explained to mean that she considered herself a second mother for her students.

Reflection

- What is your understanding of the metaphors the teachers used:
  - teacher as octopus
  - teacher as imparter of knowledge
  - teacher as moulder
  - teacher as mother
- The context of the above scenario may have played a role in the type of metaphors the teachers used. For example, the teacher as imparter of

knowledge was used to explain why English language teachers must provide content knowledge for their students so that they can pass examinations. Obviously, in other contexts where examinations do not play such a significant role, second language teachers will use different metaphors that help them form such judgements about such educational issues. What metaphors are most used by teachers in your context?

7 Classroom communication

Chapter Outline

Introduction

Classroom communication, that is face-to-face communication and interaction between teachers and students, cannot be easily controlled by a teacher because it is shaped by moment-to-moment actions and interactions within that classroom (Johnson, 1995). That said, teachers tend to follow established patterns because they have for the most part, subconsciously set up various rules by using language that performs two functions simultaneously: to carry the message that a teacher wants to communicate while at the same time, to convey specific information about who the teacher is, and whom he/she is talking to. Because teachers are often unaware of what communication patterns exist in their classes and may not know how to examine them, this chapter explores how language teachers can reflect on the communication patterns in their classrooms.

What the research says

Research on teaching in mainstream classrooms and second language classrooms suggests that the following classroom communication pattern is the most usual (or unmarked) in many classes regardless of subject content (Johnson, 1995): the teacher initiates something (**I**), a student or students usually respond (**R**), and then the teacher usually evaluates (**E**) the student response, the *IRE* sequence. The following example (from Farrell, 2004b) illustrates this unmarked underlying communication structure that can be found in a majority of language classrooms:

    1: Teacher: What time is it?   [Initiation]
    2: Student: It's 2pm.   [**Response**]
    3: Teacher: Good. *It's* 2pm.   [Evaluation]

In turn 1 the teacher asks the students for the time and wants the student to supply the actual time and the contracted *it's* for *it is*. The student responds in turn 2 with the correct contracted form *it's*, and the teacher positively evaluates the response in turn 3 with *good*, and repeats (with emphasis on it's) the student's earlier response. This brief exchange shows how a teacher uses language to manage and control classroom communication. Outside classrooms, it is unusual to find participants in everyday conversations evaluating responses to solicits; rather, participants usually acknowledge such solicits. In fact, research by Belleck *et al.* (1966) has revealed that nearly one-third of all teachers' moves while teaching consist of evaluating their students' responses.

Additionally, research has shown that in second language classrooms the teacher tends to do most of the talking (teacher talk) and one aspect of teachers' talk that has been investigated in depth is that of speech modifications made by second language teachers. Research results indicate that teachers simplify their talk to non-native speakers and that these modifications seem to make the language easier to comprehend and that this in turn facilitates acquisition (Pica, Young and Doughty, 1987). Pica and Long (1986) studied the speech of experienced and inexperienced second language teachers in terms of its complexity, question types, the functions of questions, statements, and imperatives, and comprehension checks and requests for clarification which make comprehension easier for language learners. Apart from the discovery that experienced teachers tended to use a wider range of question forms, there were few other speech differences between experienced and inexperienced teachers while teaching.

One aspect of teacher talk that is important for second language teachers to reflect on is their use of questions in class. Research has shown that 60 per cent of the time a teacher talks in class involve questioning of some sort, and of these teacher questions, most are questions are of the type that the teachers know the answers to, or display questions as in a lockstep *IRE* teacher-led sequence rather than referential questions where the teacher does not know the answer (Long and Sato, 1983). Farrell (1999b) confirmed these findings where the teacher, who was teaching a listening comprehension class in which students have to listen and watch a video tape of a current affairs programme, learned from the results of a Seating Chart Observation Record (SCORE) analysis (see Chapter 11 for examples of SCORE charts) that she had in fact asked 45 questions in a 50-minute class. All of these questions were display-type questions where the teacher knew the answers to each of the questions she asked. The teacher reflected after hearing this: 'Until now I had no realization about my questioning pattern'. Consequently, Long and Crookes (1986) trained teachers to ask more referential questions but discovered that the use of display questions by the teachers produced more student turns, the referential questions elicited longer responses and mastery of lesson content was greater in classes where teachers used more referential questions. Beliefs play a role in the way a second language teacher talks in class (Richards and Lockhart, 1994). For example, if a teacher believes that his or her students require comprehensible input from the teacher in the target language, then the amount of teacher talk time will greatly increase in the classroom. However, if a teacher believes that his or her students will learn best by using the target language, then learner talk will increase more than teacher talk. Consequently, language teachers should be aware of the impact of the following:

- The underlying communication structure in the classroom – if the communication follows the unmarked IRE structure or if there is a variation at any stages of the lesson.
- The impact of underlying communication structure of the communication in the classroom.

- How students follow what is required from them in lessons.
- The function of teacher talk in the classroom such as the teacher's use of:
  - *praise*
  - *instructions*
  - *speech modifications*
  - *use of comprehension checks*
  - *feedback*
  - *questions – the number, type and functions of questions*

Language teachers may not realize that two types of teacher talk predominate in many classrooms, exploratory talk and final draft talk (Barnes, 1976). When teachers use exploratory-type speech they are not giving the final word on an issue in that they are admitting that they do not know all the answers. A type of tentativeness characterizes their type of exploratory talk where they may be seen to be rearranging their own thoughts as they speak. They do not use a type of language that emphasizes their authority as the expert on the topic at hand which is characteristic of final draft talk. As Barnes (1976: 108) maintains, 'Final draft language is the contrary of exploratory'. Whereas exploratory speech is represented by detours where the teacher is hesitant to give a definite answer or evaluation, final draft talk is more polished in which the teacher follows a direct IRE sequence; he/she initiates, the students respond and the teacher evaluates. As mentioned in a previous chapter, research has shown that teachers mainly evaluate rather than respond (a characteristic of final draft speech); however, if teachers evaluate rather than reply they, as Barnes (1976: 129) suggests, implicitly devalue the students' knowledge and his/her 'ability to contribute to the lesson'.

Case study I: teacher questions

This case study examines teachers' use of questions in a university language class in Surabaya, Indonesia (Farrell, 2004b). The researcher audio and video recorded the classes over a six-month period seeking answers to questions such as how long EFL teachers wait after asking questions, to what extent each type of question influenced the students' participation and what the teachers did when they did not get their required responses to the questions. The class consisted of 28 students. After the student attendance was checked, the teacher asked the students about the assignment she gave the week before. It was about verbs not commonly used in the 'ing' form for the present continuous tense. Some students were asked to write the verbs on the blackboard; then the teacher asked the students to check themselves with the book. No feedback was provided for this part. The teacher went on discussing the theory about the present continuous tense vs. present simple. The transcript centres on the teacher providing feedback on student' work and only shows the following turns that are also analysed: 1–9; 27–44; 77–82; 119–33; and 168–85.

Turn		
1	T:	OK...let's go to the exercises. I suppose it's easy for you. Let's start from one student and...
2		he or she points to another student as usual. Number 2. Richard, start from you.
3	S:	Richard is going to the cinema.
4	T:	Richard is...Sorry?
5	S:	is going to...
6.	T:	Louder, please.
7	S:	Richard is going to the cinema.
8	T:	is going to the cinema. Is Richard in the cinema now?
9	Ss:	No.
27	T:	Jenifer.
28	S:	Denise is having lunch with Ken.
29	T:	Denise is having lunch with Ken. Is he having lunch now?
30	S:	No.
31	T:	No. Next
32	S:	Aini
33	T:	Aini
34	S:	They are coming to the party.
35	T:	They are coming or going or attending?
36	S:	Coming....
37	S:	Going...
38	T:	Ya. They are going to a party. OK go on to 26.2. One student takes 2 numbers. Next.
39	S:	Fani
40	T:	Fani
41	S:	Are you working next week?
42	T:	Are you working next week? Is it? Yes. Number 3.
43	S:	Tini
77	S:	I'm going to the...
78	T:	I'm going to the supermarket. I'm going to the supermarket tonight.

79	T	Can you make another . . . sentence without 'go'?
80	S :	'I'm sleeping tonight'
81	T :	Without 'sleep'
82		[Laughter] . . . not with a similar answer that has been used by your friends.
119	T:	My parents are going on holiday next week. Good.
120	S :	Oh, that's nice. Where did they goes?
121	T :	Where . . .
122	S :	do they go?
123	T :	Have they gone?
124	S :	They are going.
125	T :	Where . . .
126	S :	are they going?
127	T :	Where are they going? You cannot use 'do they go'. Ya because it's not a timetable.
128		Bukan jadwal bukan schedule /It's not a schedule/. Lima, five, number five . . .
129	S :	Rani.
130	T :	Rani.
131	S :	Silvia is doing an English course at the moment. The course finishes on Friday.
132	T :	The course finishes on Friday. Why do you use simple present here?
133	S :	A schedule.
168	T:	OK. What are you doing on Monday afternoon? What are you doing?
169		You agree we will use present continuous there. If I answer I work on B, is it possible or not?
170		You may mention I'm working because your sentence is . . . started with present continuous, right?
171	S :	Yes
172	T :	But if I use simple present in B 'I work' can I? Can I? So you're not so sure.
173		OK, let's take a look on the next page. We haven't decided yet.
174		haven't got the answer for number 10. Please move to [the] following pages on. 97 point B, fourth dot . . .
175		titik yang keempat . . . ya B titik yang keempat. Part B [page] 97 the fourth dot.
176		see page 97 part B find the explanation on the forth dot/What explanation did you read there?
177		Have you found it all?
178	S :	Yes. 1

179	T :	Yes. Ya, it is said that . . . simple present can be used also to refer to future action in this case
180		that the action is fixed like a timetable. OK let's go back to the previous page.
181		96 number 10. So what do you think? Is present continuous the only choice?
182	Ss:	No.
183	T :	No, so you can use also . . . Present. Simple present because your schedule of working is . . .
184		fixed already that you can start your work on Monday as usual. Ya, OK *The teacher goes on with the next page explaining the theory.*

Key: T = Teacher; S = student; Ss = students.

The analysis of this transcript reveals that out of a total of 14 questions, the teacher asked eight display-type questions (nearly 60 per cent of the questions), two referential questions, two clarification questions and two confirmation-type questions. Display questions included: turns 8, 29, 43, 132, 172, 176, 181a, 181b; referential, 78, 177; clarification 35, 169; and confirmation 123, 170.

Case study I reflection

➢ What percentage of the time does the teacher seem to be talking in the transcript above? Compare your finding with that of the research you read above.

➢ Is the teacher's percentage of referential questions excessive or about normal considering what you read above in the research section?

Case study II: exploratory talk or final draft talk?

Case Study II outlines an excerpt from part of an elementary school English language class (grade 5) in Singapore (Farrell, 2004b). At the end of the lesson, the teacher wanted the students to be able to list five methods of writing an introduction to a composition and apply one of the five methods to write an introduction for a given picture composition.

Turns 1–9
1: Teacher: Why do you say it's past tense?
2: Melvin: It's better we make more mistakes.

3: Teacher: It's better you make more mistakes ok, but I think most of you will use past tense because in composition, we were told to use er . . . past tense, right? Because it tells us something in the past. But for dialogue.

[*Silence*]

4: Teacher: Eh. . . . What about punctuation marks?

5: Bernard: Include commas.

6: Teacher: Yes, you have to include a comma, the open inverted commas. Very good and you should be careful in the sense that you have to place all your punctuation marks correctly at the right place. Ok? For example here, comma must come first before the close inverted commas and not the other way round, you see. So you have to be very careful in your punctuation so that you will not make eh . . . punctuation.

[*Silence*]

7: Teacher: We have 'Dialogue', we have 'Flashback' 'What, Where and When'. We have 'Description of Surroundings'. The last one?

8: Leonard: About weather. Sunny . . .

9: T: About weather. That is 'Description of Surroundings' already. Ok, one more. Last one? Think.

An analysis of the classroom talk throughout the lesson indicated that it was mostly final draft talk. What the students said and how it was said was actually a final presentation for the teacher's approval. However, there were some instances of exploratory talk too. For example, in Turn 2 the response from the student 'It's better we make more mistakes' sounded quite vague since the student did not specify what kind of mistakes. In this example, the teacher encouraged the use of exploratory talk as seen from the question posed in Turn 1. In fact, in turn 1 the teacher seemed to withhold direct correction but tried to provide sufficient prompting so that the students could perform self-correction. The students were not required to give their own opinions. They could also predict that even if their responses were wrong or insufficient, the teacher would 'help' them correct the mistakes entirely or even help them to expand on their answers. Some examples could be seen in turns 3, 6 and 9.

Case study II reflection

➤ Do you think the students understood the concepts being taught at the end of the lesson? Why or why not?
➤ Did the students have many opportunities for self-correction?
➤ What problems might teachers face if they use exploratory talk exclusively in their classes?

From research to practice

Language lessons are different from other content lessons in two main ways, the first relates to the way lessons are structured and the second the way language is used in the classroom. Richard-Amato (1988) suggests that the format of second language lessons is different from other content lessons because the same concepts may need to be reinforced time and again using different methods, especially for beginning and intermediate level students. The format of a language lesson according to Richard-Amato (1988) can be structured into five parts or phases.

1. The *perspective or opening* first phase of the lesson is where the teacher uses various procedures to orient the students such as giving a preview of a new reading lesson that he/she will teach. This opening stage of the lesson is often marked by changes in the teacher's voice quality or volume, their use of formulaic language to help signal the beginning of these events and/or in the teacher's location or posture.

2. The second phase of a language lesson, the *simulation* phase, is where the teacher poses a question (or questions) to get the student thinking about the coming activity.

3. The next phase of a lesson, called the *instruction–participation* phase, is where the teacher introduces the main activity of the lesson. During these two phases different teachers will follow different formats for lessons as they divide their lessons into sub-activities using different transitions between each activity (Richards and Lockhart, 1994).

4. The *closure* phase is where the teacher attempts to get the students' input regarding what they have learned in the lesson that was just presented.

5. The *follow-up* and final phase has the teacher using other activities to reinforce the same concepts and introduce new ones. Classroom communication research thus highlights that success of the class in terms

Table 7 Long and Sato's taxonomy of the functions of teachers' questions

1. Echoic	a. *comprehension checks*	All right? Ok?
	b. *clarification requests*	What do you mean?
	c. *confirmation checks*	Did you mean?
2. Epistemic	a. *referential*	why didn't you do your. . . . ?
	b. *display*	What's the opposite of up?
	c. *expressive*	It is interesting, isn't it?
	d. *rhetorical*	Why didn't I do that? Because . . .

of student learning necessitates that teachers and students be on the same wavelength in their understanding of what is required (Richards and Lockhart, 1994).

Rivers (1981: 486) has said that language lessons should 'contain certain familiar routines in order to serve adequately as vehicles for new information'. Different teachers sequence lessons in different ways depending on the overall goal of the lesson. For example, regarding the internal structure of many lessons, some teachers build in familiar routines that include doing something before the activity (pre-), doing the activity (during) and doing something after the activity (post-). When students know what they are supposed to do each day without having to spend too much time working this out each day, they can better focus on what they are supposed to be learning.

Teacher questions

Language teachers use questions as one of their main sources of seeking feedback that their students are learning. Different taxonomies have been developed to describe and understand the different types of questions language teachers ask in class.

Table 7 shows Long and Sato's (1983) taxonomy of the functions of teachers' questions. This taxonomy separates between the *echoic* question type which seeks repetition or confirmation of something and the *epistemic* question type which asks for information of some sort. We can compare the referential and display questions in this epistemic section with the open and closed type of questions that Barnes (1976) has talked about; they are similar but not the same as display questions, which test the students' knowledge, although they can be *closed* and referential questions *open*, the opposite is also possible for both. Not only are the type of questions a teacher asks important, so also are the way teachers ask questions during their classes. Teachers have several options available when asking general questions in class. One option is to ask the whole class a question and have students self-select when to answer. Students can vie for the teacher's attention by putting their hands up, by shouting out the answer (although not recommended in many teacher education courses it has its purposes especially if some of the students are shy then the pressure may be off them to answer in public – can you think of other purposes for which you may want students to shout out the answer?). Also, teachers can call on students who do not raise their hands to see why they think they cannot answer the question. It may be that they know the answer but they may not want to answer in public. Teachers also have the option of calling a student's name first and then asking the question. This alerts the student that a question is coming his/her way: 'Suzie, what do you think?'. Of course, if a teacher calls the student's name first, then he/she cannot be sure the student is following. So, another strategy may be to ask the question first and then call a student's name. This way, teachers can monitor if a student has been following the lesson. After asking the question, teachers must wait for their students to answer. This does not always happen and many students have been socialized into waiting *before* suggesting an answer, as many teachers will provide the answer just to fill in the silence. Cazden (1988) maintains that teachers wait at least three seconds after asking the question to allow students to think before doing anything.

Classroom communicative competence

Johnson (1995) reminds second language teachers that our students come to our classes from backgrounds that may be different from that of the main-stream education system. This is especially true in multicultural societies because the students' first language, linguistic background or learned ways of talking may be different from the language of the school and teachers must be aware that this difference (especially if the interaction patterns at home are very different from those expected in the school) may play a big influence on the quantity and quality of the students' learning. For example, research on classroom communication on the role of culture on turn taking by Philips (1983) discovered that Indian students' (from the Warm Spring Reservation in Oregon, USA) unwillingness to participate in class activities was not because then had an inferior IQ, or were overly shy; rather, Philips suggested that it was a result of how the class activities were organized. Teachers must therefore ask themselves if there are any discontinuities between the languages of the home from which their students come each day and language and inter-action norms of the classroom in which they teach. They must ask themselves what the learned ways of talking is in their own classrooms so that none of their students will be disadvantaged. Therefore, it is the teacher's responsibility to adjust instructional practices to the competencies of the students – what are the teacher's frames of reference about the students, their cultural beliefs, the status and expectations of the teacher? According to Johnson (1995) the teacher should be supportive, and use verbal and instructional scaffolds in order to make classroom events predictable for the students so that the students know what to expect and what is expected from them. Johnson (1995) further suggests that teachers must *define* their students classroom communicative competence (CCC), *establish* it and *extend* it. Johnson (1995: 160) defines classroom communicative competence (CCC) as: 'Students' knowledge of and competence in the structural, functional, social, and interactional norms that govern classroom communication'. Richards and Lockhard (1994) talk about the related concept of learners' interactional competence which looks at how they understand the rules of classroom interaction. This derives from the learners' ability to understand classroom etiquette for appropriate interaction and is influenced by culture such as use or not of a teacher's first name in class, students encouraged to speak out or not in class, how to interact in group work collaboratively, knowing how to get assistance and feedback, when to challenge what the teacher and/or peers say and other such norms of interactional competence.

The key to language teachers understanding the importance of classroom communication, and how this either sets up or blocks opportunities for their students' learning, only takes on real meaning when teachers themselves investigate and reflect on the communication patterns in their classrooms (Farrell, 2004b). That is, teachers must gather concrete data about the communications that exist in their classrooms and then use the information garnered from this data to make informed decisions about their teaching (Farrell, 2004a). The most important type of data a teacher should obtain is in the form of classroom transcripts. The teacher collects this type of data by placing a tape recorder and/or video recorder in his/her classroom. However, it may not be necessary to transcribe the entire recording as teachers can decide what aspect of the classroom communications they are interested in knowing more about. Fanselow (1987) has suggested that transcriptions be made at certain intervals or at special events that the teacher wants to investigate. For example, teachers may be only interested in reflecting on the impact of their verbal instructions in their classes, so all they need to do is to listen and transcribe those parts in the tape that show the teacher giving instructions and then the immediate turns after this (for about five minutes) to see what impact these instructions have had on their students' learning. Other topics could include the type and frequency of teacher (and student) questions, how tasks are set up in their classes, or the type of language in use in group discussions (for more details on the topics teachers can reflect on in their classrooms, see Farrell 2004b). After transcribing the classroom communication, the teacher can then analyse and interpret the data.

Reflection

➤ What does classroom communicative competence mean to you?
➤ Discuss your understanding of etiquette for appropriate interaction in your context. For example, what is involved for students in terms of group work, challenges and receiving feedback?
➤ What format have you developed when sequencing activities in your lessons?
➤ Does this format reflect any methods you have been trained to use from your teacher education courses or modifications of these methods?
➤ Do you vary your lessons? If so, how? If not, why not?
➤ How many questions do you ask in a normal class? How do you know?
➤ What kind of questions do you usually ask? How do you know?
➤ What is the function of the questions you ask?
➤ What is your wait-time after asking a question? How do you know?
➤ Philips (1983) characterized verbal interaction in Anglo-American classrooms as organized in one of four participant structures. Compare these four characteristics of verbal interaction in the classroom to the verbal interactions that exist in your classroom:
   1. Teacher interacts with all students (*most common*) – teacher controls who will talk, and when, and voluntary class participation is through self-nomination and/or compulsory participation through teacher nomination.
   2. Teacher interacts with small groups of students (*also common*) as in reading groups where the students' participation is generally the result of teacher nomination and required individual performance.
   3. Students work individually at their desks and the teacher is available for student-initiated interaction.

4. Small group activities for completing specific tasks with indirect supervision by the teacher (*more common in higher grades*).

➢ Conduct your own action research project on one of the following:
   o Will increase of the use of referential questions rather than display questions stimulate students to use more complex language?
   o Can I set up a project to stimulate and monitor the amount of student talk?
   o How will dividing my class into smaller groups which are more responsive to learner needs improve the quality of learning in my classes?

Conclusion

Classroom communication differs from normal everyday communication in that its main purpose is to instruct and inform. Classroom communication may seem to be haphazard but it is in many cases, highly regulated and ritualized. Reflecting on the patterns of classroom communication that exist in a language teacher's lessons can provide useful information that can help to further legitimize actions and confirm preconceived insights. As language teachers the only real concrete evidence we have that a lesson has occurred is a recording and transcription of the communication that represents the moment-to-moment communications between the teacher and students and between students themselves that occurred during the lesson. By reflecting systematically on classroom communication, language teachers can make more informed decisions about their teaching that are based on information obtained from analysis of transcripts of that communication.

Chapter scenario

A native-Chinese-speaking teacher was teaching non-Chinese speakers in the USA how to talk about animals in Chinese. (I thank Jerry Gebhard for this example.) The teacher was interested in exploring the communication patterns in his classes and so he decided to audio record one of his classes. The lesson starts with the teacher asking a general question to the students with an eventual lead into the topic of the 'Zoo' which takes about two minutes. The class then learns how to ask questions in Chinese such as 'What is this?' 'What is that?'. He transcribed the first 13 turns in his lesson opening to see how he oriented his students, and then the first 13 turns in the main instructional phase of his lesson which outline how the teacher taught the students how to say "turtle" in Chinese.

Lesson opening

Turns 1–13

Teacher: When you were a kid, did you wish to go anywhere? Lisa?

Lisa: Kennywood.

Teacher: Doonsoon?

Doonsoon: Korea.

Teacher: Korea? No. When you were a child, you were a kid.

Doonsoon: I'm sorry, I didn't follow you.

Teacher: What is your favourite place?

Doonsoon: (Silence)

Teacher: Phew! How was your childhood?

Teacher: How about Bill?

Bill: My grandma's.

Teacher: Ah – ok. Yeah, when I was a kid, I liked to go to this place. (shows the picture). What is this?

Chungwen: Zoo

Instruction phase

Turns 1–13

Teacher: (Showing a picture of turtle) Jen, what is this?

Jen: A turtle.

Teacher: Yeah. What about in Chinese?

Class: (laugh)

Teacher: In Chinese . . . (shows the phonetic transcription)

Class: *Guei*

Teacher: *Guei*

Class: *Guei*

Teacher: We don't have turtles in zoos?

Lisa: You can find out in aquarium.

Teacher: Aquarium?

Lisa: There are some turtles in the zoo in some areas

Teacher: Uh – ok.

In the opening of the lesson it seems that the teacher asks open-ended questions but not all of the students were able to follow the topic of these questions (e.g. turns 3–9). In fact, the teacher wants to 'guide' the students to an answer he has in mind because the content of his lesson is talking about animals in Chinese. In the opening phase transcript in turn 1, the teacher was not really interested in getting an answer such as Doonsoon answered as she responded 'Korea' and not the Zoo. Also, in turn 10, the teacher is trying to elicit the answer 'Zoo' from Bill, and so did not respond when Bill answered 'Grandma's' in turn 11. Rather, the teacher finally showed the class a picture of a Zoo in turn 12 and asked the class what the picture signified. Chungwen provided the correct answer. In the instructional phase transcription the teacher wanted to teach the students how to say 'turtle' in Chinese. It may seem that the question in turn 3 is a display question, but according to the teacher, it was not as he knew that Jen (an American) would not be able to answer it as the teacher said that this type of question 'usually could make the class laugh'. It is interesting that after teaching the students how to say the word 'turtle' in Chinese, he then asked referential questions referring to turtles and that they are in the Zoo.

Reflection

- What kind of questions did this teacher use mostly in class and what were the functions of these questions?
- In the opening phase it is possible that Doonsoon did not understand the question and it is also possible that Doonsoon really wanted to go to Korea, but the teacher wanted to steer the discussion towards the topic of zoos as Chungwen finally answered. What is your understanding of the classroom transcript in these opening turns?
- Get together with a colleague and record and transcribe the communication in your classes. Next, analyse (and compare) your lessons for one or all of the following:
  - The underlying structure of classroom communication.
  - Variations in the underlying structure.
  - How the academic task structure was set.
  - Analysis of the social participation structure.
  - How many and what kind of questions were asked.
  - The type of language evident in group work.
  - What overall patterns can you see in communication structures in your classroom and in your colleague's classes?

8 Action research

Introduction

Action research generally involves inquiring into one's own practice through a process of self-monitoring that generally includes entering a cycle of planning, acting, observing and reflecting on an issue or problem in order to improve practice. Wallace (1991: 56–7) maintains that action research can have a 'specific and immediate outcome which can be directly related to practice in the teacher's own context' and is 'an extension of the normal reflective practice of many teachers, but it is slightly more rigorous and might conceivably lead to more effective outcomes'. As mentioned in Chapter 1, systematic reflection means that language teachers collect data about their teaching so that they can make more informed decisions about their teaching; however, whereas reflective teaching can result in non-observable behavioural changes in the classroom such as increased levels of awareness of a teacher's assumptions, beliefs and practices, conducting an action research project usually results in some kind of transformation of the research into actual and observable actions. This chapter outlines and discusses how reflective language teaching can be facilitated through conducting action research.

What the research says

Within second language education, action research has usually been associated with the study of classroom actions rather than addressing social problems associated with language teaching. Bailey (2001: 490) maintains that action research for language teachers is 'an approach to collection and interpreting data which involves a clear, repeated cycle of procedures'. Action research is conducted by practising language teachers because they themselves are valuable sources of knowledge regarding their own classroom situations and as a result change can be implemented more credibly because practising teachers will find the results more credible and valid for their needs. However, action research is different from usual research conducted by academics, and while academic research is valuable in its own terms, it often has little practical application for practising teachers. As Sagor (1992: 3–4) has observed: 'The topics, problems, or issues pursued [in academic research] are significant, but not necessarily helpful to teachers on the front line'.

Examples of actual action research abound in the English language teaching literature in recent times and teachers who have carried out action research often report significant changes to their understanding of teaching. Gow, Kember and McKay (1996) working in Hong Kong, for example, focused on encouraging independent (student) learning at the tertiary level, and reported improved student learning as a result of their action research project. Another interesting study conducted by Curtis (2001), who encouraged 20 Hong Kong teachers to carry out small-scale action research studies which focused on how they could increase and improve the quantity of spoken English used by their learners in their English lessons, also reported positive results from partaking in action research such as increased teacher awareness of classroom dynamics, and expectations of their learners. In addition, Curtis (2001: 75) reported that the teachers learned 'a great deal about themselves, their students and their teaching and learning environments through action research'. Stewart (2001: 79) carried out action research to explore how Japanese university students use questions in formal debates and concluded that action research for language teachers is not only a way to solve problems 'but it is found in the very act of entering into the cycle of investigation'. Stewart (2001: 87) maintains that action research 'forces teachers to think about what they are doing in the classroom in a systematic way through a lens focused on one particular area of their practice'. The literature on action research for language teachers suggests the following:

- It involves collecting information about classroom events (in the classroom), through observation or through collecting information in other ways, such as through interviews, questionnaires or recordings of lessons.
- It involves careful and systematic collecting of that information.
- The research involves some kind of follow-up action.
- This action involves some change in practice, and monitoring the effects of such change.
- The results are owned by teachers, rather than the research community.
- The results of the research can be reported at a staff meeting or through a written report.
- It seeks to build up a knowledge base about teaching based on practitioner's knowledge, rather than expand the knowledge base developed by academics and theoreticians outside of the school context.

Among the goals of action research therefore are the following:

- To develop research skills useful for classroom inquiry.
- To bring about changes in classroom teaching and learning.
- To develop a deeper understanding of teaching and learning processes.
- To empower teachers by giving them the tools which they can use to further impact changes within the profession in which they work.

Case study: correcting grammar

The following action research project was conducted in Singapore. By comparing and contrasting the teachers' beliefs (see Chapter 3 for more on beliefs) about grammar correction together with their actual practices, the researchers wanted to see whether there was a discrepancy between beliefs and classroom practices while assessing grammar in student written work (Farrell and Lee, 2003). The two Chinese female teachers who had volunteered to participate in the action research project actually initiated the study. They had been interested in how they were correcting grammar and if they were in fact doing what they thought they were in their classes. So they were eager to participate in this action research project for their own professional development.

Both researchers first read up on the topic of grammar correction. The action research (AR) project utilized data-collection methods such as classroom observations, teacher interviews, student interviews and collection of writing samples of students' work. All the observations were tape-recorded, transcribed and analysed. The recorded responses from the teacher interviews were also transcribed to find out what teachers claimed to do in the area of grammar correction in compositions. The results of the observations indicated that that both teachers had a tendency to correct every grammatical error in their students' written work. They also showed an alignment between their perceptions and actual assessing practices in terms of types of grammatical focus. That the two teachers corrected every grammatical error was a bit of a concern because the literature on grammar correction questions the efficacy of attempting to identify all errors in students' compositions. We mentioned to the teachers that Ur (1996) has suggested selective correction because it may not be possible for students to learn from their errors thoroughly in oral or written work because they will not be able to cope with the sheer quantity of information. However, we also realized at this stage in the action research process that if the teachers are to implement changes in their beliefs about correcting all grammatical errors in their writing, it may take some time. Consequently, we suggested to the teachers that in future they could set aside class time to persuade the students of the effectiveness of selective error correction and the futility of correcting every grammatical error. They said they would introduce this into their writing classes.

Case study reflection

➢ Why do you think it may be a good idea to read up on a topic before conducting action research?
➢ Can you think of other ways the above action research project could have been conducted?

➤ Do you think the action research project outlined above seems complete? Why or why not?

➤ Do you think every grammatical error in your students' writing should be corrected? Why or why not?

➤ What grammar correction techniques do you use when assessing your students' written work and why?

From research to practice

When teachers want to conduct an action research project they enter into a cycle of investigation that includes the following steps:

1. *Identify an issue*
2. *Review literature on issue and ask questions to narrow focus of issue*
3. *Choose method of data collection*
4. *Collect, analyse and interpret information*
5. *Develop and implement and monitor action plan*

Identify an issue

According to Bailey (2001: 490) the action research cycle begins when 'the researcher decides to address a problem, investigate an issue, or pose and answer questions in his or her own context'. Selecting an issue is probably the most important and most difficult part of the action research cycle because it involves considering a number of practical considerations that must be kept in mind such as limiting yourself to one issue or problem, usually an issue that you are really interested in and that will have a positive impact on your class or on your teaching. Wallace (1998: 21) suggests that when selecting a topic and purpose for action research the following points should be considered:

1. *Purpose*: Why are you engaging in this action research?
2. *Topic*: What area are you going to investigate?
3. *Focus*: What is the precise question you are going to ask yourself within that area?
4. *Product*: What is the likely outcome of the research, as you intend it?
5. *Mode*: How are you going to conduct the research?
6. *Timing*: How long have you got to do the research? Is there a deadline for its completion?

7. *Resources*: What are the resources, both human and material, that you can call upon to help you complete the research?

A large number of interesting general issues are available for language teachers wishing to reflect on their practice through action research including (but not limited to) the following:

- *Teaching the four skills* (issues relating to changes in the way aspects of reading, writing, listening or speaking are taught in your class).
- *Classroom dynamics* (issues related to the kinds of interaction which occur in the language classroom).
- *Learner language* (issues relating to the kind of language that is generated by specific activities your students use when completing classroom discussions and the amount of language they produce during pair or group work).
- *Grouping arrangements* (issues relating to how different grouping arrangements such as pair, group or whole class, promote learner motivation, language use and cooperation).
- *Use of materials* (issues relating to different ways in which materials are used and how these affect the outcomes of lessons).
- *Grammar and vocabulary* (issues relating to the teaching of grammar and vocabulary and the effect of using different teaching and learning strategies).
- *Assessment policies and techniques* (issues relating to the forms of assessment you currently use in your classes and their outcomes).

Review literature and ask questions

After deciding the focus of the topic of interest for action research, teachers can start reading some background literature on the topic. Although Burns (1999: 192) maintains that 'referring to the literature should be a matter of choice' and Wallace cautions that busy teachers may not realistically have time to read, reading about what others have discovered before can give teachers more ideas about how to conduct their own action research projects by following similar research methods or adapting the methods used for their own contexts. For example, in the case study outlined in this chapter the interview questions used to gather information were adapted from a review of the literature on error correction. Five fundamental questions about error correction were chosen in the case study interview:

1. Should learner errors be corrected?
2. If so, when should learner errors be corrected?
3. Which learner errors should be corrected?
4. How should learner errors be corrected?
5. Who should correct learner errors?

Also at this stage teachers can decide whether they want to explore the issue alone or with other teachers who are interested in the same issue. In this regard, Burns (1999) insists that teacher collaboration is a vital aspect of action research because of the sharing involved in every aspect of carrying out the research from the practical to the emotional support.

Choose method of data collection

The teacher next plans and decides on a strategy to collect data now that the problem has been identified and even read up on. Burns (1995) maintains that in action research projects, the data collection methods most commonly used and most appealing to second language teachers draw on qualitative and ethnographic methods and techniques and these usually include some combination of the following: careful and systematic collection of information about classroom events through interviews, observation, field notes, questionnaires, recordings (audio and video) and transcriptions of lessons. Among other methods, Burns (1995: 8) suggests the following approaches to collecting classroom data:

- *Journals/diaries*: regular dated accounts of teaching/learning plans, activities and classroom occurrences, including personal philosophies, feelings, reactions, reflections, explanations.
- *Teaching logs*: more objective notes on teaching events, their objectives, participants, resources used, procedures, processes, outcomes (anticipated and unanticipated).
- *Document collection*: sets of documents relevant to the research context, e.g., course overviews, lesson plans, students' writings, classroom materials/texts, assessment tasks/texts, student profiles, student records.
- *Observation*: closely watching and noting classroom events, happenings or interactions, either as a participant in the classroom (participant

observer) or as an observer of another teacher's classroom (non-participant observation). Observation can be combined with field notes, recordings and logs or journals.

- *Field notes*: descriptions and accounts of observed events, including non-verbal information, physical settings, group structures, interactions between participants. Notes can be time-based (e.g., every 5 minutes) or unstructured according to the researchers purpose.
- *Recording*: audio or video recordings, providing objective records of what occurred, which can be re-examined. Photographs or slides can be included.
- *Transcription*: written representations of verbal recordings, using conventions for identifying speakers and indicating pauses, hesitation, overlaps and any necessary non-verbal information.

Of course, there are advantages and disadvantages to each of these forms of data collection and it is most important that the information collected is reliable in that the procedures that are used measure accurately what they claim to measure. One way to ensure this is to collect information from several different sources about the issue under investigation. For example, in the case study outlined in this chapter, the researchers decided to triangulate their data collection by using classroom observations that were recorded and transcribed, teacher interviews that were recorded and transcribed, a number of student interviews that were also recorded and transcribed and a collection of writing samples of students' work, and lesson plans (document collection in the above list) as well as the researcher's written-up log of not only classroom observations but all interactions during the action research project in order to get the best understanding of the issue under investigation. In the case study, the last stage in data collection involved collecting two pieces of graded compositions from each student that included the students' corrections. One of the compositions completed before the action research project started, and the other composition the most recently assigned when the action research began. The rationale for collecting a composition completed before the research began was to check whether there were any discrepancies between teachers' usual habits and their practices during the period of research. While collecting the writing samples after the action research began served as evidence for the teachers' actual correction practices. In addition, the student interviews were used to supplement data collected from the writing samples so that more detailed information could be elicited.

Collect, analyse and interpret information

Once the data has been collected, the teacher then analyses and reflects on it and makes a data-driven decision to take some action. Wallace (1998: 21) maintains that teachers can also think about changing or refocusing their original research question at this stage: 'As you proceed with your research, do you suppose that you will have to rethink your original question?' As a general guide the goals at this stage of action research are:

- To identify patterns in the data.
- To compare findings from different sources of data.
- To build an interpretation from the information collected.

The main purpose of this stage is to make meaning of data gathered in order to determine the value of the intervention and involves sorting through the data to discover important themes relating to the issue under investigation. For example, in the case study reported in this chapter responses from the teachers' interviews were transcribed and analysed to find out what the teachers claimed to do in the area of grammar correction in compositions and their underlying rationale for their perceived actions. The teachers' claimed practices were then verified through an analysis of their correction techniques as observed in the collected writing samples (the analysis of the writing samples only focused on grammatical errors that the two teachers had spotted). Recorded tapes and field notes from classroom observations were also used to confirm (or deny) the teachers' claimed practices in giving grammatical feedback. If data from the analysis of teachers' correction techniques in the writing samples and the classroom observations supported the responses made in the teacher interviews, this was regarded as an alignment between beliefs and practice. On the other hand, if data from the analysis of teachers' correction techniques in the writing samples and the classroom observations contradicted the responses in the teacher interviews, this was considered as a discrepancy between beliefs and practice.

Develop, implement and monitor action plan

The final steps in the cycle of action research is reflection in terms of deciding on some type of action, monitoring the effects of that action and, if necessary, problem redefinition. Teachers ask themselves at this stage what it all means for them and the result of this reflection usually involves some change in teaching practice which is monitored. Eventually, the whole cycle can begin again as the teacher redefines the problem in light of the findings of the first cycle. For example, in the case study reported in this chapter, the findings revealed that both teachers corrected every grammatical error they could find in their students' compositions. They also showed an alignment between their beliefs and actual marking practices in terms of types of grammatical focus possibly because of their common dislike for selective marking. Although most students said they believed that they could benefit from grammatical feedback in their compositions, only 50 per cent of them wanted their teachers to correct every grammatical error in their writing. We relayed these findings to the teachers and also that research indicates that correction of every grammatical error does not positively contribute to students' improvement of grammatical accuracy in their composition and that more selective grammar correction on students' written compositions might be more beneficial for students for their language development. The teachers told the researchers that they would implement the suggested changes including using more selective correction of grammar in their students' writing and also explain to the students why they were going to make these changes by citing not only the findings of the action research but also the findings of the literature reviews.

The overall best and simplest way to decide if an issue you are considering qualifies as action research is to ask three questions about the proposed study and if the answer to all three is 'yes', then it fits under an action research umbrella, but if the answer to any is 'no', then action research may not be an appropriate approach:

1. *Is the focus on your teaching action?*
2. *Are you in a position to be able to change your future actions (teaching and otherwise) based on the results of your action research project?*
3. *Is improvement possible?*

Thus action research as it is outlined in this chapter can be not only enjoyable but also rewarding for teachers and it is viewed as a cycle of activities rather than a one-step response to a problem. It is a natural extension of a teacher's classroom activities because it can be conducted by teachers in their own classrooms. As Burns (1999: 183) maintains, action research can help to 'build a community of practitioners aligned towards teacher research and a professional climate that is open to public scrutiny and constructive critique'.

Reflection

➤ What is your understanding of action research and have you ever conducted an action research project? Explain.

➤ Why do you think academic research generally has little impact on practising teachers? Do you think there is a gap between academic research findings and practice in the classroom? Why or why not?

➤ In what ways can conducting action research empower a second language teacher?

➤ In what ways can conducting action research develop a collaborative relationship with other teachers?

➤ Do you think the results of the action research project should be reported, e.g. at a staff meeting or through a written report to a journal? Explain.

➤ Wallace (1998) discusses how an interest in a topic such as *group work*, must be thought through to find a more specific focus for classroom investigation. Can you add any more to the list developed by Wallace?
  ○ how to set up groups
  ○ how to form groups
  ○ how to resolve personality clashes within groups
  ○ how to deal with the use of the mother tongue during group work
  ○ how to select materials for group work
  ○ how to assess the effectiveness of group work

Conclusion

Action research serves the needs of the reflective professional well because it combines the mastery of the professional knowledge a teacher has built up over the years with the wisdom of everyday practice. Although there is no one universally accepted set of processes that constitute conducting action research, it is generally agreed that it focuses on researching an issue of interest to the teacher and usually takes place inside the classroom to determine what is currently occurring. Action research involves the teacher systematically collecting information about this issue and then acting on the information to make improvements to the issue. In order to help teachers collect information related to their action research project, they can use such reflective tools such as teaching journals, classroom observations, narrative analysis and group discussions among other methods that are all covered in this book. Through a process, then, that includes planning, observing, analysing, acting and reviewing, language teachers can learn a great deal about the nature of classroom teaching and learning as well as acquire useful classroom investigation skills.

Chapter scenario

Joan is a native-English-speaking teacher from the USA and has just arrived in Korea to teach English in a university language institute. Before this she was teaching English for academic purposes (EAP) courses in a university institute in the USA. Her students came from various different cultures and were more than likely going to attend (or were attending) college. She has an MA in TESOL from an American university. When she arrived in Korea she started teaching oral proficiency courses (called conversation classes) in a language institute attached to a university. This was the first time she had taught students from the same cultural background (Korean). She was given various classes from beginning level to advanced level. Joan was the type of teacher who continuously asked her students if they were following the lesson and if they could understand her. She continued this practice in her classes in Korea. So she was surprised one day when the director of the institute (a Korean professor) called her into his office after her first month of teaching to tell her that all her beginning students complained about her teaching methods and her speed of speaking in the class. They also complained that she was constantly drinking coffee during her classes. She was shocked because the students had never complained to her directly and they had always told her that she was a great teacher when she asked if they understood the lesson. Joan had always had her coffee cup with her in her classes in the USA and the students would come to her if they had any problems. Joan decided that she would conduct an action research project on this topic of culture difference and she started by reading more books on Korean culture. She noted the vast and subtle differences between the cultures of the USA and Korea in general terms and in terms of teaching in a university institute. Next Joan decided that she would have to adapt several new strategies to check if the students were following her lessons, and if she was acting in a culturally appropriate manner in her classes. She decided to carry out the following strategies and activities:

- Not to take a yes answer as evidence that the students were following her lessons.

- To build in quizzes into every lesson to check if the students really understood what she was teaching.
- To try to build up relationships with the students after class time.
- To find out how Korean teachers conduct their classes (by observing their classes).
- To hold several classes on topics related to cultures: Korea and the USA.
- To talk to more experienced native-English-speaking teachers in the institute and try to set up some peer coaching type collaborations.
- To team-teach some classes with native-English-speaking teachers and Korean teachers.
- To keep a teaching journal and note instances where there could have been a cross-cultural mix-up.
- To self-monitor her classes more carefully by recording some of her classes.

Joan enacted most of these activates over a two-month period and built up a wealth of information and knowledge about teaching EFL classes in Korea. After about three months, Joan became more comfortable teaching in this new culture and her students began to see what a concerned teacher she really was. Joan could have become a bitter EFL teacher and blame her students, the institute and the new country for her initial problems. Instead, being the professional that she is, she examined her situation and carried out her own action research analysis of the problem and, as a result, developed her understanding of different teaching circumstances.

Reflection

- What do you think of the strategies Joan attempted?
- Outline some more strategies Joan could implement to help her solve the dilemma this case presented her.
- The general stages (cyclical) of the action research process outlined above are: (1) *plan* (issue identification), (2) *research* (literature review), (3) *observe* (collect data), (4) *reflect* (analyse and interpret) and (5) *act* (redefining the problem).
  - How can you advise Joan to implement such a cycle of action research for the problem she faced above?
  - What difficulties do you anticipate Joan may face in carrying out action research using this cycle? How could these difficulties be resolved?

Teaching journals 9

Introduction

Teaching journals are another means language teachers can use to reflect on their practice. Teaching journals provide teachers with a written record of various aspects of their practice such as classroom events and enables them to step back for a moment to reflect on their work. When teachers write regularly in a teaching journal, they can accumulate information that on later review, interpretation and reflection can assist them in gaining a deeper understanding of their work. This chapter explores how and why regular journal writing can help language teachers reflect systematically on their work.

What the research says

Although the role of writing as a method for language teacher reflection has not been widely acknowledged either positively or negatively by language educators

(Burton, 2005), what little research exists nevertheless mostly suggests that journal writing can help language teachers (both beginning and experienced) think about their work. Ho and Richards (1993: 8) maintain that journal writing can be an 'opportunity for teachers to use the process of writing to describe and explore their own teaching practices'. McDonough (1994: 64–5) observed that experienced teachers who wrote regularly about their teaching became more aware of 'day-to-day behaviors and underlying attitudes, alongside outcomes and the decisions that all teachers need to take'. More specifically, Jarvis (1996), who analysed the content of journals written by practising language teachers that were intended to promote reflection in an in-service course, discovered that journal writing benefited language teachers in the following ways: as a problem-solving device, for seeing new teaching ideas and as a means of legitimizing their own practice. In addition, Seaman, Sweeney and Meadows (1997) noted the positive effects for busy teachers of reflecting with the aid of teaching journals.

Bailey (1990: 218) suggests that a teaching journal can be a place for language teachers 'to experiment, criticize, doubt, express frustration, and raise questions' about their practice. When this form of journal writing is performed alone by a language teacher, it has been called an *intrapersonal* journal because the teacher writes solely for himself or herself (Gebhard 1999). However, the research of Brock, Yu and Wong (1992) suggests that practising language teachers can benefit more from having others (peers) read their journals (once issues of trust and confidentiality have been agreed upon) so that they can get another's perspective, insight and interpretation that may be difficult to achieve if a teacher attempts to reflect alone. As Brock, Yu and Wong (1992: 300) discovered, collaborative journal writing 'raised our awareness of classroom processes and prompted us to consider those processes more deeply than we otherwise have'. The research of Keiko and Gaies (2002) has indicated that it is possible and probably more desirable for language teachers to combine both intrapersonal journal writing and peer sharing of journals where one teacher can first write an intrapersonal journal and later share it with a partner who can read and comment on the journal entries noting patterns and issues that can be discussed. Teachers can also work in pairs or in a teacher development group and decide on a single topic in which each participant will write about and then later share their writing. Consequently, the research suggests that journal writing for teachers can serve the following purposes:

- as a way of clarifying one's own thinking
- as a way of exploring one's own beliefs and practices

- as a way of becoming more aware of one's teaching styles
- as a way of monitoring one's own practices
- in order to provide positive feedback on one's teaching, for example by writing about successful experiences
- to vent one's frustrations and set goals for remedying problems
- to raise questions and issues to think about in the future
- as a way of collaborating with other teachers in exploring teaching issues
- as a way of triggering insights about one's self as a teacher and about one's teaching
- to provide a record of one's teaching for others to read

Collaborative journal writing for peers while incorporating all of the above benefits for individual teachers can also serve the following purposes:

- as a means of encouraging reflective enquiry
- as a means of challenging, supporting and monitoring the teacher's thinking
- as a means of asking questions
- as a means of analysing the teacher's development, learning and current levels of understanding
- as a means of guiding instruction
- as a means of linking and synthesizing the teacher's understanding with his/her classroom practices

Case study: three EFL teachers write about their teaching

This case study reports on three English as a foreign language (EFL) teachers who met weekly in South Korea to reflect on their practice (Farrell, 1998a). All three teachers were experienced EFL teachers in Korea. Initially, all three teachers agreed to write an ongoing journal account of their experiences during the semester of reflection. They agreed to write at least one entry after an 'event' was experienced; an 'event' was to include a class observation and/or discussion, and a group meeting.

At the end of the semester of reflection each teacher's journal showed a different focus of reflection. For example, T1, out of a total of 22 entries in one semester, was mostly concerned with evaluating her teaching. She frequently cited problems, both personal and teaching-related, that influenced her teaching. One such difficulty she wrote about concerned the issue of how and when to correct her students' language errors. In an early journal entry she addressed this issue when she was considering how to correct a pronunciation class: 'One of my weakest points is voiced sounds like [z] in zoo or museum. But I'm not an English native speaker, too'. In contrast to T1, T2, was the most prolific of the three teacher-writers with 28 entries over one semester, and used the journal to focus his reflections on theories of teaching. For example, he wrote about how he as a language teacher makes a decision about how long to wait after asking a question in class and what the research says; he continued: 'We must extend the wait time before we make a decision as long as we can stand the uncertainty, as we extend it waiting for a student response. This is what makes teaching a buzz anyway, the uncertainty. Which is what Lortie was writing about in *The Schoolteacher*, which I'm reading now'. T3 was the least active of the three teachers in her journal writing and had only six entries after the semester. In fact, T3 said that she stopped writing in her journal completely after a few weeks because she noted that writing 'gave me stress, I always had to write something down, but I didn't have anything to write'.

Case study reflection

➤ T1 in the case study outlined above wrote about her concern about how and when to correct her students' language errors. Have you ever been concerned with this same topic? If yes, what did you do about it?

➤ If you have not reflected on this topic before, write a journal entry on how and when you correct your students' language errors.

➤ What are your theories of teaching and who or what has influenced them? Where do your theories of teaching originate?

➤ T2 was interested about the amount of time he should wait (wait-time) after asking a question. How long do you usually wait after asking a question before you resume talking if students do not answer?

➤ In the case study of experienced EFL teachers outlined in this chapter, the three teachers agreed to write for one semester and after an event of interest. Do you think one semester of such journal writing is a sufficient amount of time for reflection? Why? Why not?

From research to practice

Language teachers can start writing a journal as soon (if they have not done so before) as they start their first job; however, even experienced teachers who have never written a teaching journal can start anytime and start reflecting and investigating various aspects of their work. It is not always easy to start writing a teaching journal because some teachers may not know where to focus their reflections. Bartlett (1990: 209) says a teacher can start to write about our 'conversations with pupils, critical incidents in a lesson, our personal lives as teachers, our beliefs about teaching, events outside the classroom that we think influence our teaching, our views about language teaching and learning'. So there are many possible topics to choose from specifically focused concerning: group work in class, giving of instructions, the use of teacher questions, giving feedback/correction of errors, to more macro concerns such as: lesson planning, textbook selection, curriculum development, administration influences. The following procedures may be useful when starting a teaching journal for the first time:

- Start a teaching journal (if you have not already done so).
- Reflect on a recent teaching practice or experience in the classroom, positive or negative, that *caused you to stop and think about your teaching.*
  - What happened before this incident?
  - What happened after it?
  - Why was this incident important for you?
  - What does this incident tell *you* about *you* as a teacher?
- Write this (word processing or on paper).
- Decide whether you want this to be an intrapersonal journal or a dialogical journal.
- After each journal entry ask yourself two or three questions about what you have written. Your peer may respond to these questions.
- Keep writing about your chosen topic for at least a month.
- Review your entries each week. Can you find any patterns emerging?
- If you have chosen an intrapersonal journal, write a summary of important events and what you have learned.
- If you have written a dialogue journal, decide on what parts of the text you want your peer to read (block text, staple pages together that you do not want made public, or write a different version for your peer).

By writing a teaching journal for a month, the reflections can thus be spread over a period of time and this allows teachers to observe patterns and trends that they may not ordinarily see. In order to achieve this focus it is best to set boundaries to help you pinpoint a focus for more inquiry by disciplining yourself to write each week and for 15 minutes each day for that period. It may be an idea to respond to the same prompts for each entry as the participants in the case study outlined in this chapter decided like: 'What did you notice in your classes this week?' and 'What professional issues are of interest to me today?'. In this way the participants in the case study outlined above also created some manageable boundaries for themselves because all responded to the same prompt each entry although their topic choice was different. All three teachers then decided to share their journals with each other by photocopying them but no comments were written or made on each of the journals. Alternatively, some teachers may already have issues that they consider important for them to explore by writing.

After writing for some time, teachers can look for patterns they may see emerge in their entries and when they have noticed a pattern, they can investigate it in more detail by engaging in an action research project that critically explores whatever theme or pattern has emerged. Many teachers may never have had the experience of writing about their own teaching and may wonder about what form of writing they should use, how much to write and for how long they should write before they stop to analyse their writing. In the beginning, teachers should write regularly about a topic for at least a month while at the same time reviewing their entries each week. At the end of the month it may be a good idea to write a summary of some of the important events that arose and what has been learned as a result of the reflection process. Later teachers can increase the period of writing as they become more comfortable with the writing process as a means of reflection. In terms of the appropriate style of writing, Richards and Farrell (2005) have suggested that language teachers can use a *stream of consciousness approach* or an *edited* approach when writing a teaching journal. When writing a 'stream of consciousness' form of journal, teachers should remember that grammar, style and organization are less important than obtaining a written record of teaching acts and a teacher's feelings and thoughts about those teaching acts. This type of exploratory writing can generate lots of ideas and awareness that can be examined later and analysed for recurring patterns of events. The following is an example of a stream-of-consciousness type of journal entry from one of the teachers in the case study reported on in this chapter.

When my students took a seat face to face with me most of them looked nervous. So I started with 'How are you today? How was your exam?' to make them relax. But on the contrary it backfired. Some of them were panicked by my unexpected questions. So I stopped to do that and got to business right away. In fact, I meant to comment on his grammatical problems but I changed my mind. Because I, as teacher, made many mistakes, too. I felt whenever I opened my mouth I was making a mistake. Nevertheless our communication worked. Isn't that our aim to learn a language? Besides, I don't want to dampen cold water on his enthusiasm to practice English.

When writing for another teacher peer a more edited writing style may be the best approach (although the peer could also overlook grammatical errors) and written entries by the peer can be made directly on the journal. In this way, the teacher can decide what to include in the journal for the peer to see and what to leave out. Richards and Farrell (2005) suggest the following general format for such journals:

- **Date and time of entry**: a journal entry should be written on the day of the event if possible, otherwise you may forget details of what happened and when.
- **Sequencing of the events**: to help you record what happened and when, it is best to make a brief list describing what happened before, during and after the event.
- **Elaboration of details**: describe the event that happened in detail and add how you felt at the time these events happened.
- **Analysis of the event**: try to explain what you think the event's significance is for you. What did you learn? Did the event raise more questions than provide you with answers? Try to figure out what you have accomplished and how you plan to follow up on what you have learned.

The following is an example of an edited teaching journal (adapted from Richards and Farrell, 2005):

March 16th, 2:30–3:30.
Sequence of Events:

- started class as usual
- went over homework
- noticed that most students did not do the homework
- was annoyed and frustrated

Events:

We (the class and myself) went over the grammar exercises (articles, *a*, *an* and *the*) that I had given for homework (because they always make many mistakes in articles in their writing) for the first fifteen minutes. I had tried to make these grammar exercises interesting for the students by provding handouts that challenged their knowledge to (a) recognize that there was a grammar mistake and (b) try to give the correct answer. I have found that my students are so used to doing the fill-in-the-blank-type grammar exercises that they do not have to think about why there may be a mistake. So, my main reason for providing a passage with all the English articles omitted was to get the students thinking about their knowledge of grammar (recognizing that there is a mistake in the first place) and then correcting that mistake. I hope they will use this system in their peer editing of compositions too.

Episode:

After about ten minutes in which I was going around the class asking the students for their answers, I noticed that many of them had not done their homework. I was very disappointed because I had spent a long time preparing this homework sheet (handout) and I had thought long and hard about how I wanted to teach articles to these students because of the quantity of mistakes in their written and oral work. I felt really annoyed that these students did not appreciate the work I was doing for them or that fact that they were not motivated enough to correct their misuse of articles in their writing and speaking. This never really happened in any of my classes before.

Analysis:

At this stage I can't really say that I came up with any clear solution to the problem. Was it that they were just not motivated to study grammar or articles in particular? Was this the reason they all did not complete their homework assignment? Or was it because they did not know how to complete the assignment? Maybe they are not used to this sort of grammar assignment (first find the mistake and then correct it). Maybe it is because they were used to filling-in-the-blank-style-exercises? I think I should have explained this type of grammar exercise in more detail and show them why it is very useful for their grammar development. On reflection, maybe I should have done more of these article exercises during class. I was really surprised at their level of resistance to this type of homework. I now realize that by writing this down, I have a clearer picture than when it happened in class with all the associated emotions. But it was a bit of a shock for me because students would always tell me if they had not understood something before. Anyway, I just went on to another topic. I will return to the topic of articles in English grammar next week and explain why this type of grammar exercise is useful and how they can use this in their peer editing during composition classes.

Additionally, teachers should consider whether they should or want to share their journals with other teachers (and even their students!) or keep them private. If teachers have written a journal to share with their peers, they can decide on what part of the text they want their peer(s) to read. If they do not want a peer to read a particular part of a journal, they can block the text they do not want made public by stapling or gluing pages together, or they can simply write a different version (a summary) for peers to read. For example, in the case study outlined in this chapter, T3 could have omitted the entries she did not want the other participants to read rather than abandoning her writing and thus reflections.

Now the internet offers more scope for teachers to share their teaching journals on a wider scale. An example of this is a new approach to keeping *online teaching journals* and *blogs*. Towndrow (2004: 175) used a laptop to keep an 'electronic journal-cum-diary' to record his own reactions and observations of his students' learning during a course and found this form of reflective journal writing very successful. In addition, Siemens (2004) has recommended that teachers become involved in *blogging*, defined here as a format which is constant (archives, links, time stamps, chronological listing of thoughts and links), personalized, community-linked, social, interactive, democratic, new-model innovation built on the unique attributes of the internet. Among other uses, Siemens (2004) suggests that *blogs* are useful for self-expression and knowledge sharing and management and as he suggests for 'free flow – any idea can be expressed . . . and accessed by any one'. The reason why *blogs* have taken off so fast is that they are relatively easy to get started with and language teachers can share them easily with other teachers because they are your story.

Journal writing is not necessarily something all teachers enjoy or think is useful. Richards and Ho (1998) for example, in a survey of 32 teachers' evaluations of their experiences of writing a journal, found that 71 per cent of the teachers found it useful, 25 per cent found it fairly useful, while only 4 per cent did not enjoy writing a journal. Here are some things language teachers said about journal writing:

What teachers liked about it:

- Writing a journal forces the teacher to reflect on certain issues and bring them out in the open.
- Journal writing gets teachers thinking about things that are unconsciously going on in the mind.

- Journal writing enables receptive teachers to discover the importance of relating their own experience of learning to that of the pupils they teach.
- Journal writing enhances awareness about the way a teacher teaches and a student learns.
- Journal writing serves as a means of generating questions and hypotheses about teaching and the learning processes.
- Journal writing is the most natural form of classroom research.
- Journal writing promotes the development of reflective teaching.

What teachers did not like about it:

- Writing a journal is time-consuming.
- Writing a journal can be artificial unless it is a regular activity.
- Comments by peers can be unfocused.
- Journal writing can become tedious after some time.
- Journals can be difficult to analyse and interpret by teachers, peers and teacher educators.
- Some writers really do not enjoy writing a journal or diary as a form of reflection.

Obviously journal writing takes time: time to write and time to read (and time to analyse and make interpretations). So, a major decision one has to make concerning journal writing is how many entries to make (frequency) and what length (quantity) each entry should be. Concerning the reading of journals, peers and/or groups of teachers could read the journals at the start of every meeting, and this would be easier if the journals were emailed to participants before each meeting. In addition, some teachers may require special training in journal writing. Teachers could be given models of effective journal writing and asked to follow these models if they are uncomfortable with their own way of writing.

Reflection

➤ Do you enjoy writing? If yes, why. If not, why not?
➤ Have you ever written a teaching journal? If not, why not?
➤ If yes, what kind of entries did you make? How often did you make them? Was this journal an intrapersonal journal for yourself or a dialogue journal for other teachers to read and comment on?

➤ Discuss Jarvis' (1996) findings that journal writing can benefit language teachers in the following three ways: *as a problem-solving device, for seeing new teaching ideas and as a means of legitimizing their own practice.* Do you agree with these findings? Why? Why not?

➤ What general topic would you like to start writing about?

➤ How will you write? Will you use a pen and paper and/or computer and/or use a blog?

➤ Compare journal writing using a notebook (pen and paper), a computer or record in an audio recorder. What are some of the advantages and limitations of each way of keeping a journal?

➤ Which type of journal do you think will be most effective for your needs, a stream-of-consciousness type or a more edited type as outlined above? Explain your answer.

➤ In a dialogue journal, a peer responds to journal entries through discussion or through written entries. What type of responses from a peer would you like to see written in your dialogue journal? What type of responses would you write to a peer in such a teaching journal?

➤ Recently, there has been an increased interest in the use of 'blogs' and 'weblogs' as a means of writing a teaching journal for publication. What do you think are the advantages and disadvantages of these ways of keeping a teaching journal?

➤ How long do you think is the ideal duration for writing a teaching journal so that you can begin to see patterns in your practice that give you insight into your beliefs, assumptions and practices? Explain your answer.

Conclusion

Language teachers can write teaching journals to record their reflections of most aspects of their practice and review later for patterns that may have emerged as a basis for reflection. It is this very process of writing that helps teachers to consciously explore and analyse their practice (Shin, 2003). Of course, and as the results of the case study presented in this chapter suggest, writing may not be suitable as a means of reflection for all teachers for different reasons such as fear of revealing one's reflections in writing, and even difficulty with the writing process itself but, it is to be hoped, with practice, they may change their minds. That said, for the majority of language teachers research has indicated that writing about one's practices seems to be an efficient means of facilitating reflection. The added advantage of writing a teaching journal is that it can be shared with other teachers. When teachers share their reflective journals, they not only foster collegial interaction but they can also gain different perspectives about their work while also contributing to professional knowledge in the field as a whole.

Chapter scenario

John, an ESL teacher in the UK decided to write about his reflections on the student evaluations he just received concerning teaching English as a second language in a small university language centre. He wrote the following in his teaching journal after he received these evaluations: 'I just got my student evaluations today and I was surprised to see that out of 40 evaluations (20 for each semester), some of the students thought that they were not improving their English language speaking ability and that I was not correcting them enough when they thought they had made mistakes. Apart from that, they all seemed satisfied that I was doing a good job. I think that they link my lack of corrections to their perceptions that they are not improving in the speaking ability, but I am pushing fluency over accuracy. I guess I will have to explain this more and why I do not interrupt them in mid-sentence even if they make a mistake. I follow my own rule: If the mistake does not interfere with the overall meaning of the sentence, then I think it is fine. I do, however, point out mistakes if I see a pattern of common mistakes in a student's speech, but only at the end of the class. Actually, I write them down when the student makes these mistakes, so I must show the students exactly what I am doing about this. I must also ask them how they expect to improve as a result of taking a short conversation course (2 hours per week, for 12 weeks)'. He decided to continue with his journal writing the next semester to monitor what would happen with his students, their learning and their evaluations of his teaching.

Reflection

- Try to finish John's reflections on the student evaluations as if you were him.
- Write about your own reflections on the most recent evaluations your students have given you.

- Choose one (or more) of the following issues relating specifically to English language teaching and explore them through journal writing first in an intrapersonal journal and then share your writing with a peer in a dialogue journal.
  - Classroom management problems such as having too many students in one class and how to conduct a class while still maintaining control.
  - Problems with too much teacher talk and not enough student talk in the target language.
  - Problems with students who continuously speak in their native language during class and make few attempts to speak in the target language.
  - Problems with students who speak too much in class and do not give chances to others.
  - Problems with different cultural groups within one class.

Teacher development groups

10

Chapter Outline

Introduction

Since the day they started to teach, teachers have been socialized to work in isolation from their colleagues and this has led to feelings of insecurity because teachers may be afraid to share their experiences with other teachers for fear of being 'exposed.' However, if teachers come together on their own initiative in order to reflect on their work, they can complement individual members' strengths, and compensate for each member's limitations, all for the common good of the group and the institutions in which they work. As Little (1993: 138) has pointed out, one principle of professional development for language teachers is that it can offer 'meaningful intellectual, social, and emotional engagement with ideas, with materials, and with colleagues both in and out of teaching'. This chapter outlines and discusses how teachers can work together when they volunteer to join a teacher development group to form relationships with colleagues in order to discuss, share and reflect on their beliefs and practices both inside and outside the classroom.

What the research says

Teacher development groups provide a context where participants can reflect on and come to understand their classroom practices, and plan their professional growth and development together in a safe place. Head and Taylor (1997: 91) define a teacher development group as 'any form of co-operative and ongoing arrangement between two or more teachers to work together on their own personal and professional development'. Teachers as well as other members of a school (or teachers from different schools) come together in such groups or networks in order to improve their teaching and their students' learning through collaboration on the basic assumption that collaborating with a group of colleagues will be more effective than reflecting alone. Research suggests that collaboration is an important component of teacher professional development because it involves teachers sharing their personal and professional knowledge with other teachers. As a result of participating in teacher development groups, teachers can change their thinking about their work and as a result can become more confident practitioners (Matlin and Short, 1991).

Research indicates that language teacher development groups facilitate dialogue, sharing and collaboration and the exchange of resources, information and expertise. For example, after realizing that they have been pursuing their own professional development in isolation for several years as individual language teachers, three language teachers in the USA decided to come together in a teacher development group not only for the purposes of reflecting on their practice but also as a means of offering 'hope to others wishing to break out of the shells of isolation separating teachers from their colleagues as well as from teacher educators' (Oprandy, Golden and Shiomi, 1999: 152). Oliphant (2003) has observed that language teachers join a teacher development group in order to pursue professional development, because individually they can only do so much such as attend conferences, read the literature on language teaching and self-monitor their teaching. She also noted that teachers can become empowered through teacher development groups because they benefit from working together with other teachers. Teachers become empowered because they become more confident in themselves and their work as a result of group membership and they begin to question the so-called experts as they gain more experience in the group (Matlin and Short, 1991). For language teachers then the research suggests the following advantages and benefits to working in teacher development groups:

- The group can generate more ideas about classroom issues than can any one individual.
- Within the group there is a variety of levels of expertise allowing novice teachers to learn from the experience of experts.
- A group provides supportive social relationships for its members.
- A group provides a non-threatening environment in which teachers can develop new knowledge and skills and gain supportive feedback from peers.
- A group provides an opportunity for language teachers to help other teachers face and overcome dilemmas relating to their practice.
- A group of teachers working together can achieve outcomes that would not be possible for an individual teacher working alone.

Case study: language teacher development group in (inter)action

This case study reports on a language teacher development group in Korea (Farrell, 1999a). The participants met for 12 group meetings where each group meeting was planned for one hour, but usually lasted two hours. At the first meeting all were told that it was up to each participant what topic or topics they wanted to reflect on during the project and that all discussions within the group would allow for equal sharing of power by all group members.

The most frequent topics that the teachers talked about in the group meetings included their approaches and methods to teaching and learning, their theories of teaching, how they evaluated their teaching, and their self-awareness of themselves as teachers. They were most interested in talking about descriptions of their teaching methods, procedures and class content, while relying on classroom experience to guide these practices. They also seemed to be quite concerned about the school context, both inside and outside the school, as well as concerned about their learners. Their discussions of theories of teaching centred on personal opinions, with little justification for these theories expressed and little or no evidence of application of these theories to classroom practices.

In addition, all three teachers evaluated their teaching in terms of problems they encountered. For example, T2 said at the second group meeting that the feeling he gets from class is 'not about what I think I should be. I want to feel good about teaching, but I don't. There must be a perfect way for teaching for everyone'. Another pattern evident in the group meetings was the limited discussion on teacher self-awareness and few questions about teaching. When the participants did talk about these issues, it was mostly about perceptions of themselves as teachers, and in the form of asking for advice, respectively.

Case study reflection

➤ Have you ever participated in a teacher development group such as the one outlined above? If yes, explain. If no, why not?
➤ If your answer to the above question was yes, explain how you got together, how long the group lasted and what you all talked about.
➤ If your answer to the above question was no, do you see advantages or disadvantages to starting a teacher development group similar to the one outlined above?
➤ Why do you think the most frequent topic they talked about in group meetings concerned their approaches and methods of teaching and learning?
➤ Why do you think the teachers did not talk so much about their self-awareness of themselves as language teachers?

From research to practice

Types of teacher development groups

Generally, there are three main types of teacher development groups and they can extend not only within the school but may span several schools or school districts as well as other organizations: *peer groups* can be set up within a school, teacher groups can be set up at the district level, *district-level groups* and *virtual groups* that can be formed anywhere.

School peer groups

Language teachers can set up a peer network within one school such as an English-language group made up of all the English language teachers in the school/institution (Sitamparam and Dhamotharan, 1992). The committee can decide on specific activities designed to provide the individual teacher avenues to develop in whatever ways he or she wants and needs.

District-level teacher groups

Peer networking can also operate outside the school and within a school district. Teachers can set up a central coordinating committee that integrates activities and communicates with the teachers. Special-interest groups such as a writing teachers' group can carry out activities in the district related to their area of interests. For example, a group of teachers interested in teaching writing can come together to decide the best ways to introduce more process-type writing activities into the curriculum of that particular school district. This group then communicates with the central coordinating committee who supports this writing teachers' group in terms of providing resources, and contacts with other districts to consult what they have done on this topic to advise the group. They can also provide logistical support such as places where the teachers can meet regularly for meetings.

Virtual teacher groups

Virtual groups of language teachers such as TESL-L can of course be set up anytime as they can easily communicate and 'interact' on the internet. One of the positive aspects of these virtual groups is the willingness of many professionals within the field to offer advice and good-quality information free of charge to teachers from all over the world. Many of these groups provide easy instructions on how to join and members receive regular communications via emails. One of the drawbacks (apart from the vast amount of emails these groups generate) of these virtual communities of language teachers is that since the vast majority of the participants have never met, some professional teachers may feel they are users (not contributors) of the group just gathering up all the information without putting anything back into the group. One free electronic journal, TESL-EJ, also exists on the internet as a forum for language teachers to publish their research (http://www.kyoto-su.ac.jp/information/tesl-ej/index.html).

Forming teacher development groups

Starting a group

Teacher development groups are built on a foundation of shared understandings which is developed and nurtured by projects that involve members of the group in meaningful interaction with each other. Richardson (1997) has suggested that when colleagues come together in a group to reflect on their work, four basic features or ingredients need to be present if the group is to be successful:

1. Each participant needs to feel 'safe' within the group. This means that the group must be seen as a place where each participant is able to open up and experiment as they discover who they are personally and professionally.
2. Each participant needs to feel 'connected' in some way or other.
3. Each participant has to have a sense and to be able to feel passionate about the group and what they are trying to accomplish together. For this to happen, they must feel that they as a group are making a difference of some sort.
4. Each participant must honour, and be grateful for the group's existence. This sense of group solidarity blends the other three features mentioned above.

The above four features were important for the participants in the case study reported in this chapter when they were starting their language teacher development group. In fact, they sought each other out originally not only for their own professional development, but they were also seeking the camaraderie of working together as a group. Nevertheless, all three had different purposes for coming together as a group. They were each concerned with the isolation of their various roles as teachers in Korea but all wanted to probe deeper into their teaching and their students' learning processes.

Participants' roles

Once a group of teachers decides that they want to form a teacher development group they must then figure out how they want to operate such a group in terms of members, roles, topic setting and general rules of the group. Each teacher study group is composed of members with different roles; one of the most important being the group's leader. Kirk and Walter (1981) suggest a democratic approach, where the leader should not attempt to manipulate the group into doing what he/she wants. It seems that when groups have leaders, these group leaders may face a dilemma between getting the task completed, while at the same time maintaining good relations with and among group members. That said, group leaders must be able to create a trusting environment by encouraging and acknowledging the contributions of all members so that any individual is not allowed to dominate the group discussions. However, it may also be possible for a teacher development group to have a type of co-existing leadership in order to provide more opportunities for getting the task done (one co-leader) and maintaining group cohesion (another co-leader) as developed in the case study reported in this chapter. Regarding roles of individual members in a teacher development group Belbin (1993) suggests individual members tend to be predisposed towards one or more natural roles in the group as follows:

- *Coordinator* or *facilitator* who makes a good chairperson and ensures that everyone in the group has an opportunity for input.
- *Shaper* who drives the group forward.
- *Implementer* who gets things done.
- *Monitor evaluator* who ensures that all options are considered.
- *Team worker* who helps cement the group together.
- *Resource investigator* who develops outside contacts.
- *Complete/finisher* who finishes things off.
- *Expert* who provides specific areas of knowledge.

In the case study reported in this chapter, the group facilitator and also group shaper throughout the period of reflection assumed the group leader role at first but an aspect of change in the interaction in the group was the emergence of T2 as an alternate leader after meeting number five as the group members were beginning to become more comfortable with each other. T3 assumed the team worker mantle as well as monitor, while T3 could be seen as a plant in that she was always willing to look at issues from several different angles. One result of the findings of this teacher development group is that it may be better for future groups to be aware of and even negotiate up front all the different roles possible from the beginning rather than letting roles happen.

Deciding on topics

When teacher development groups come together for the first time they may or may not have a focus for the group discussions. Participants can first brainstorm a topic together and then narrow it down by identifying specific questions to explore. This narrowing down of a topic allows participants to focus their attention on issues that have personal meaning for them. The group can also at this stage decide if they have the resources available for them to continue reflecting on that particular topic. When the topic is temporarily exhausted, then the group can start another cycle of brainstorming a topic followed by a narrowing of the topic with development of specific questions addressing that topic. In the case study reported in this chapter the original facilitator of the group started each group discussion for the first five meetings but T2 started to set the topics for each meeting after that by the very act of starting each meeting by asking: 'what do we want to talk about this week'. From the fifth meeting onwards, different pairs or threes, excluding the group facilitator, interacted with each other.

Sustaining the group

As with any activity involving people with different personalities, backgrounds, levels of interest, experience and goals, teacher development groups can and will encounter issues that will need to be addressed. Because teaching is a very personal activity, as teachers in a group begin to open up and discuss personal and professional issues that are important to them with other teachers whom they may or may not know, there will inevitably be a certain level of anxiety present. So a non-threatening environment of *trust* should be fostered in the group. This can be done through observations and comments that keep judgements to a minimum. It is important that trust develops naturally from people caring about each other as a group in order for all participants to grow together as teachers. In the case study reported in this chapter two different patterns of interaction seem to have emerged in the group. For example, in meetings two, three and four the group facilitator was more active than the other participants, while in meetings five, seven, eight, nine, ten, eleven and twelve a different pattern of interaction developed where the original group facilitator was less involved as the other individual group members became more active. Thus, meetings one, two, three and four can be called Phase I of the group process – *the getting to know you stage*, while Phase II includes the remainder of the meetings (meetings five to twelve) – *the reflective stage*. In addition to breaking periods of silence in the first four meetings, the group facilitator also set the agenda for each of the initial meetings and set the topic of discussion for these meetings in the getting to know you stage. However, from the fifth meeting onwards, different pairs, excluding the group facilitator, interacted with each other and established the reflective stage of the group. Thus, trust was established after the fifth meeting and T2's use of language in these later group meetings and his paraphrasing of members' contributions all contributed to lowering the level of anxiety levels in the group. This, in turn, encouraged the other participants to reflect more and become more freely involved in the group discussions.

Another issue that must be considered is *time* because there is no optimum time plan that fits every group. Teacher development groups should consider that member availability can affect a group's time plans and institutional time limits may affect time factors for many groups. The teacher development group reported on in this chapter took a flexible approach which was informal for each of the activities and they did not specifically state what they wanted to achieve in each of the activities. With this level of flexibility in the group, each participant exhibited a different level of energy and time commitment. For example, two of the participants were active in all of the activities, while the other participant chose to be active in only one of the activities. This flexible approach on the one hand provided opportunities for the group to progress at its own pace, in a way which best suited each individual's own needs. However, on the other hand it appeared that at times the group and individual members within the group drifted off into their own agendas and there was always a danger that more pressing (sometimes important but mostly trivial) matters or problems would take over each participant's level of commitment. Nevertheless, once the group has begun to meet, members should have the right to modify the existing time arrangement to fit their needs. These can normally be resolved relatively easily as long as group members are committed to the success of the support group and are willing listeners. However, teachers who set up support groups should be aware that trust among the group members is very important because as teachers discuss and open up to other teachers about issues that are important to them, there will inevitably be a certain level of anxiety present. The following are suggestions that teacher development groups can consider so that they can maintain and sustain their group reflections over a period of time:

- *Commit to the group*: make time to be at each meeting, try to be on time for each meeting, and stay the course of the group reflections as a whole.
- *Negotiate ground rules*: try to work out what ground rules you want to establish for each meeting in terms of topics to be covered.
- *Assign roles*: give each group member a specific role (e.g., leader, implementer, expert – see above) and assign a task each week to each member in order to focus the discussion of each meeting (e.g. bring in a reading of interest on theory or practice of a specific aspect of language teaching to share with the group).

- *Listen to each other*: really listen to everything each member says without judgement for as long as possible so that all members have had a right to voice opinions in a democratic format, and then members should offer feedback that is supportive.
- *Look at the positives*: focus on achievements and accomplishments rather than on what is difficult to achieve in the group.
- *Agree to confidentiality early on*: decide on some way where confidentiality will be guaranteed from the very first meeting possibly in the form of a written agreement or contract stating how group members will deal with confidentiality.

Evaluating the group

After a teacher development group finishes its period of reflection it is important that all group participants evaluate the influences of the group on their personal and professional growth so that they can have some closure. They can also reflect on the group processes as a whole. Participants can reflect on whether they achieved their individual and group goals, their individual and the group accomplishments and factors that can be considered if they or others want to set up another teacher development group. Also they can at this stage consider if they want to share their findings with other teachers who may benefit from hearing about their experiences. They can attend a conference and report about their group to other teachers and they can also write up the group developments for a journal publication. Two participants from the teacher development group reported on in this chapter wrote up an informal paper that was not published about their experiences while participants in the group. They started their reflections by writing the following: 'Two members of a teacher development group seek to continue the experience by looking back at it and trying to make sense of it. Examining their feelings and regarding the experience/writing as experimental, the interpretation they put on it is personal but the implications they see as extending beyond their own experience to all TD groups. They believe the group empowered them and made them better if not more insightful teachers and that other people working in such groups can receive the same benefits. All participants said that they came together in order to become more confident teachers. Initial goals set were general in nature from wanting to reflect on their teaching from discussing theory to observing their practice. All the 12 group meetings were supportive and covered such diverse topics as general life experiences, inability to deal with large language classes, students' responses to questions in class, handling uninvolved students, material for conversation classes, giving feedback and the concept of what it is to be a teacher. The meetings lasted an average 2.5 hours each, exceeding the time participants had allocated. Because the goals of the group were not made specifically clear from the beginning, some of the participants felt they had either been unsure of the direction they were heading. They all said that they believe the teacher development group empowered them and made them better if not more insightful teachers and that they encourage other teachers to work in similar groups so that they too can receive the same benefits.'

Reflection

➢ Three main types of teacher groups were outlined above: peer networks within a school, groups within a school district and virtual groups. Discuss the advantages and disadvantages of all three.

➢ Which type of group would suit your present needs and why?

➢ Can you think of any other type of teacher development groups?

➢ Discuss Richardson's (1997) four basic features necessary for the successful formation of a group of teachers. Do you agree with these? If yes, why? If no, why not? Can you add more?

➢ Each teacher development group is composed of members with different roles. Discuss each of these roles and how they can be assigned to different members in a teacher study group.

➢ Why do you think it took five group meetings to really get going in the case study reported on in this chapter?

➢ Do you think that all teacher development groups will encounter the same two stages of development as resulted in the case study report: the getting to know you stage and the reflective stage?

➢ Time constraint is often given as the major problem when teachers want to meet in a group. Discuss how time should be addressed when forming a teacher development group.

➢ How can groups develop trust?

Conclusion

When language teachers come together in a group they can foster more of a sharing attitude with each other and can help each other to articulate their thoughts about their work so that they can all grow professionally together. Teacher support groups provide a context where its members can reflect on and come to understand their beliefs and practices, and others' beliefs and practices so that they can develop into more aware and confident teachers. Teachers as well as other members of a school can come together in such groups in order to improve their teaching and their students' learning through collaboration in which they discuss diverse topics related to such issues as teacher self-development, curriculum, teaching methodology and other aspects of a teacher's work. Teachers who join teacher development groups report that they develop a greater sense of professionalism because it allows them to live the process as learners that they wanted to create for their students.

Chapter scenario

Three teachers of English language, Jerry, Mark and Sophie, decided to come together as a group to explore strategies for teaching writing. Most of the students in the school came from a non-English speaking home environment and had below average English language proficiency, especially in writing. After approaching the school principal, Rita, to ask for school support, Jerry, Mark and Sophie decided they would go ahead with such a collaborative relationship with Sophie acting as a kind of coach to the other two: Sophie would help Jerry and Mark clarify certain issues regarding their teaching of writing in order to make their classes more effective. Rita was delighted that they had volunteered to enter into such a collaborative relationship, so she decided that she would help them both personally and administratively. First, Rita agreed that when Sophie was observing Jerry and Mark teach, she would teach their classes. Rita also made time for them in their teaching schedules so that they would be able to meet at least one time a week as a group to discuss their progress. All three teachers decided to gather information during the sessions: they would keep a written journal of their experiences, Sophie would observe Jerry and Mark teaching at least two times each week, they would hold a discussion directly after each observation, and that they would write up their findings at the end of the collaborative relationship so that other teachers could find out what went on (this last point was influenced by Rita, the principal).

Reflection

- What do you think about the way the school principal and the three teachers approached this idea of collaborating in a group?

- What do you about the way the school principal helped administratively?
- What do think about the activities they selected for the peer coaching?
- What do you think about how and when they wanted to carry out the activities they planned?
- How do you think Jerry, Mark and Sophie each benefited as a result of entering into this group arrangement?
- List the various reasons why a group of language teachers would want to come together to talk about their teaching. Which of these purposes would be the easiest to pursue? Which would be the most time-consuming? Which would be the most likely to succeed given the realities of a language teacher's busy schedule?
- What are the major factors to consider when forming a teacher development group like the one above? Rank these factors in order of importance.
- Thinking about your own particular context now, how would you form a teacher development group and who would you ask to join you in this group?
- What do you think is the best method of attracting members to a teacher development group? If you have had experience in a teacher development group, how were you and other members recruited?
- Setting up a teacher development group is not without its problems. Discuss some possible problems that could arise (e.g. when organizing the group, group size, conflict, rules, frequency of meeting, etc.).

Classroom observations **11**

Introduction

Because classrooms are such busy places, with many different activities happening at the same time, much of what is really happening in that classroom for the most part actually remains largely unknown to the teacher. By systematically reflecting on their classroom teaching and their students' learning, language teachers can develop better awareness and understanding of not only their own instructional processes but also the different agendas that are being pursued by their students. Engaging in classroom observation for the purposes of professional development can help language teachers develop more of an awareness of the principles and decision-making that inspires their teaching so that they can distinguish between effective and ineffective classroom practices

(Day, 1990). This chapter outlines and discusses classroom observations that include self and peer observation for the purposes of professional development rather than evaluation so that teachers can become more confident in knowing that they are providing optimum opportunities for their students to learn in that classroom.

What the research says

Research suggests that classroom observation for second language teachers can be unnerving for the observed teacher thus many practising teachers would rather avoid being observed by a peer or supervisor. This is because many observations are conducted by peers or supervisors who evaluate teachers with the aid of checklists comprising preconceived categories of what constitutes good or bad teaching. Williams (1989: 86) maintains when teachers are observed by peers or supervisors who use a checklist it can be 'threatening, frightening, and regarded as an ordeal'. Consequently, Williams (1989: 87) suggests that if classroom observations take a developmental rather than an evaluative approach, the teacher 'knows that the visit is not a test, but a mutual problem-solving experience' and can thus develop their critical thinking skills. In order for such developmental observations to succeed Gebhard (1999: 35) has pointed out that they should entail: 'Nonjudgmental description of classroom events that can be analyzed and given interpretation'. These descriptions can be verbal or written, depending on the purpose of the observation.

Self-observation is a systematic approach to 'the observation, evaluation, and management of one's own behavior' (Richards, 1990: 118) in order to have a better understanding of teaching and ultimately to gain better control over it. Richards (1990: 118) defines self-observation as a 'teacher making a record of a lesson, either in the form of a written account or an audio or video recording of a lesson, and using the information obtained as a source of feedback on his or her teaching'. This type of self-observation can lead to critical reflection on teaching, to 'move from a level where they may be guided largely by impulse, intuition, or routine to a level where their actions are guided by reflection and critical thinking' (Richards, 1990: 119). When classroom observations are carried out with a peer, they can lead not only to more collegiality in a school but also more self-knowledge about the type of teaching strategies other teachers use. In addition Fanselow (1988: 116) has noted that when we observe other teachers, we can 'construct, reconstruct, and revise our own teaching'.

Research has thus far indicated that classroom observations have the following benefits:

- a way of developing self-awareness of one's own teaching;
- a means of collecting information about teaching and classroom processes;
- a way of examining classroom events in details;
- a chance to see how other teachers teach;
- an opportunity to get feedback on one's teaching;
- a means of building collegiality in a school;
- an observer:
  - sees how another teacher deals with many of the same problems that he or she faces on a daily basis;
  - can collect information about the lesson that the teacher who is teaching the lesson might not otherwise be able to gather;
  - sees the teacher using effective teaching strategies that the observer has never tried.

Case study: 'What kind of writing teacher am I?'

This case study outlines how one teacher of academic writing used classroom observations with a colleague to help her reflect on her practice (Farrell, 2006c). The teacher pointed out: 'I want to have an observer's perception and interpretation of these academic writing classes'. Three main issues emerged from the classroom observations as noted by the observer: *classroom interaction, peer-response feedback* and *language medium* in her classes.

Classroom interaction

One major issue to emerge from the class observations was the teacher's interest in classroom interaction in her writing classes. The first class in this writing cycle (pre-writing) commenced with the teacher standing in front of the students (seated in rows) giving an introduction to the writing lesson. The teacher asked individual students questions in lock-step fashion (e.g., the teacher asked a question, and students answered in choral fashion (or not at all) and so on) until the end of the class. On reflection she noted that her class could, 'involve more participation from the students rather than me doing the talking which became monotonous after a short while and there wasn't any analysis of any kind of the results [of the class discussion]'.

Peer-response feedback

The teacher initiated the peer-response session during the fourth class of the writing cycle and started the class by asking the students to move into groups to answer questions on peer-response handouts. The students were asked to fill out these handouts to answer questions about their peers' composition. The students sat in groups of four, read compositions and then wrote at length on the handouts. Next they exchanged the peer-response handouts and talked to each other in Mandarin (and according to the teacher, not necessarily about their writing). The teacher noted after this class that one of her main concerns was that the students seldom talked to each other (or the teacher) about their writing after the response sheets were returned.

Language medium

The teacher said that she does not now require the students to speak in English at all times during the class. She said that she had adopted this stance only recently (the previous year) when she was reading one of her student's journals about being forced to speak English only in class. She continued: 'After reading one student's journal who felt he was giving up his Chinese when learning English I had never demanded students to use English in their discussion'.

Case study reflection

➢ Look at the three main issues that emerged from the classroom observations in the case study outlined above: *classroom interaction, peer-response feedback* and *language medium*. How do you treat all three areas in your writing classes?

➢ When asked in the post-observation interview about how she provided feedback to the students, she said that she provided feedback according to student expectations and also according to what point she wanted to emphasize during a class. She commented: 'I tend to focus more on content and organization. Previously, I tried to correct the errors when I read drafts. Based on feedback from previous students, they would like the teacher to correct their errors. So now I correct them as I spot them in the essays'. Do you think the observer should have challenged this view or not? Explain your answer.

➤ Although the teacher said that she takes a process approach to teaching writing, it was evident to the observer who has made her own interpretations about how to apply this approach to writing and this came out in the post-observation discussions: She said that this involves getting the students 'to understand the different stages a composition goes through from brainstorming to planning, drafting, peer-conferencing/peer-editing to an eventual final draft composition'. How do you think the observer facilitated the teacher to express her beliefs and reflect on her classroom practices regarding her teaching of writing?

➤ What other activities could or should the observer have done to facilitate the reflection process outlined above and why?

➤ What 'ground rules' should be built into the relationship between the observer and the observed?

From research to practice

Classroom observation can be carried out alone, as in self-monitoring, and/or in pairs (as in critical friendships) where teachers observe each other's class, and/or in small groups where teachers in a group take turns in observing each member's classes. The former is the most unobtrusive while the latter may be the most disruptive to the learning environment. Perhaps experienced teachers who have not observed their own or other teachers' classes should consider starting with their own classroom observations by looking at their own teaching. For example, teachers may not realize the following kinds of things about their teaching (from Richards and Farrell, 2005):

- Their explanations are not always very clear.
- They sometimes over-explain or under-explain things.
- They talk too quickly at times.
- Many students do not pay attention while they are teaching.
- They tend to dominate their lessons.
- They tend to speak to some students more often than others (linked to the teacher's action zone – position where the teacher is standing).

- They have some irritating speech mannerisms such as over-frequent use of 'Yes', 'Uh, Uh' or 'right'.

Consequently, self-monitoring can help teachers better understand their own instructional practices and make decisions about practices they wish to change.

Self-monitoring can be carried out through journal writing, self-reports, tally sheets and/or recording (audio and video) lessons with or without coding schemes. Journal writing (see also Chapter 9) connected to classroom observations consists of written recollections of a lesson in as much detail as possible and as soon as possible after the lesson. Of course it would also be useful for the teacher to write before the lesson about what he or she wanted to achieve in that lesson and how he or she was going to go about teaching the lesson. Then immediately (if possible) after that lesson the teacher can reflect on what he or she thought the students learned and what the lesson accomplished. By later reviewing what was written, aspects of teaching that may not have been obvious during the class may become clearer to the teacher. In addition to the teacher's written reflection, he or she can ask the students to reflect on a particular lesson by asking them to answer questions in the last five minutes of the class about that lesson such as:

- What do you think the lesson was about?
- What was easy for you?
- What was difficult?
- What activities were easy for you? What activities did you like? Explain.
- What activities were difficult? What activities did you not like? Explain.

Another method of gathering information for a teacher who is reflecting on his or her lessons is by the use of self-reports. Self-reporting allows the teacher to make a regular assessment of what a teacher is doing in the classroom and this can be done quantitatively or qualitatively. Self-reporting using a quantitative approach involves completing a checklist of some sort in which the teacher marks which practices were used during the lesson and how often they were used. The accuracy of self-reports increase when teachers focus their reflections on the teaching of specific skills and when the self-report is constructed to reflect a wide range of teaching behaviours (Richards, 1990). The following topics may be suitable for focused classroom observations and self-reports:

- *Teacher's time management*: allotment of time to different activities during the lesson.
- *Students' performance on tasks*: their strategies, procedures and interaction patterns.
- *Teacher's action zone*: the extent to which the teacher interacted with some students more frequently than others during a lesson.
- *Use of the textbook*: the extent to which a teacher used the textbook during a lesson and the types of departures made from it.
- *Pair work*: the way students completed a pair work task, the responses they made during the task, the type of language they used.
- *Group work*: students' use of L1 versus L2 during group work, students' time-on-task during group work, and the dynamics of group activities.
- *Classroom interaction*: the different types of seating arrangements that provide opportunities (or block opportunities) for more student participation and language development.
- *Lesson structure*: the nature and impact of the learning activities.
- *Classroom communication*: the communication patterns evident, including the teacher's use of questioning, which either promotes or blocks opportunities for learning.

When a teacher uses self-reports over a period of time, he or she can discover the kinds of activities he or she uses or favours, and the kinds of activities that worked well or did not work well.

Tally sheets, although they can be open to misinterpretation, are easy to use to focus on specific elements, good for self-analysis by teacher, and useful for the observer to use while watching class. The following example of a tally sheet for describing group interaction was used by a teacher group I was working with in Asia and may be helpful to get teachers started in thinking about and ultimately making their own tally sheet that best meets their particular needs and the needs of their students. The tally sheet was used to monitor small group interaction within group work where a small number of students were working together and alone; in other words the teacher was not controlling the interaction and task completion in the group. This tally sheet helped the teacher determine how the group used its time when completing a required task. The teacher coded every 10 to 15 seconds to illustrate what the group is doing at that particular moment and then looked at the pattern that emerged over the task completion time.

Task	Frequency
Discussion in target language	---------
Discussion in native language	---------
On-task discussion: general group	---------
On-task discussion: one/two dominate	---------
Off-task discussion	---------
Group silence	---------

This same tally sheet can be adjusted to monitor the involvement and participation of individual students during group work when the teacher chooses one particular student (or observes different students within one group every few minutes) from one group and observes this student every 10 to 15 seconds and makes an entry.

Teachers can also record their lesson via audio or video recordings in order to gain insights into their classrooms. A recorder (video and audio) can be placed in a strategic place in the classroom in order to capture as much as possible of what is occurring during the class. A microphone can be placed on the teacher's desk and/or on the teacher himself/herself. Teachers can also place several recorders around the room. Video recordings can later be viewed alone or with other teachers. Certain things can be done to minimize the influence and possibility of disruption of the presence of an audio or video recorder on the lesson and on classroom interaction. For example, a teacher can make lesson recording a regular feature of his or her class, even if he or she does not plan to use all of the lessons that have been recorded. This way both the teacher and the students can become familiar with the presence of the cassette and/or video recorder so that it soon ceases to be a distraction and they might even forget that it is there. Then one of the recorded lessons can be chosen for study. Freeman (1989) further suggests that when teachers choose to audiotape or videotape their lessons they should make sure the equipment is working properly before class, make notes as an activity is being recorded (e.g. while students are doing a group task) and use more than one recorder, particularly when doing group activities. When reviewing the lesson, Richards and Farrell (2005) suggest that the teacher needs to ask questions about his or her teaching that will depend on how the teacher views such things as:

- His or her role in the classroom and how he or she tries to relate to students.

- The kind of student–teacher and student–student interaction the teacher tries to encourage.
- The extent to which the teacher believes in such things as learner autonomy and learner centredness.
- The extent to which the teacher favours a direct or a more indirect teaching style.

The teacher can then consider questions such as the following:

- What did I do well?
- What did I do not so well?
- Did I learn anything unexpected about my teaching?
- What kind of teaching characterized the lesson?
- Were there ample opportunities for learning and for student participation?
- How well did I do in relation to the following aspects of the lesson:
  - ○ pacing
  - ○ explanations
  - ○ questions
  - ○ feedback to students
  - ○ creating a positive and supportive atmosphere

In terms of collecting information from classroom observations, language teachers can also use pre-designed coding schemes such as Fanselow's FOCUS – Foci for Observing Communications Under Settings (Fanselow, 1987) or SCORE – seating chart observation record (Acheson and Gall, 1987) or teachers can take an ethnographic approach (Watson-Gegeo, 1988). If teachers use a detailed coding scheme they code according to predetermined categories that are the focus of the observation and all categories hold equal importance for the teacher. In ethnographic observations data emerge only from the observations themselves. Both approaches have advantages and disadvantages and it is probably best for teachers to use both approaches rather than just one. The case study reported in this chapter used a combination of both approaches and the teacher who was being observed said that she benefited most when the SCORE was used during classroom observations. For example, Figure 11a shows the seating chart observation record (SCORE) analysis of the flow of communications during a 15-minute segment (teacher asked all 20 questions) of a first class that both observer and teacher deemed was representative of how she usually teaches academic writing; in this class it can be seen that the teacher

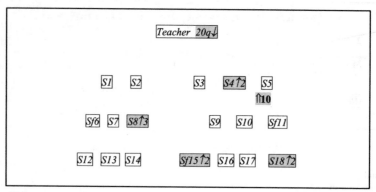

Key
Sf1↑2 = student # 1 (female) responded 2 times
20↓ = teacher asked 20 questions
↑10 = 10 choral student responses

Figure 11a SCORE analysis for interactions in Class 1

asked most of the questions and the students responded with choral or group answers.

After the class the teacher (who also examined the SCORE segment) noted that the type of interaction that had just occurred was not what she had intended, because she said that she believes that students should interact more with each other during the pre-writing stage in order to generate their own topics for writing. So the teacher later implemented these ideas the next time she started a pre-writing cycle (the seventh classroom observation in our process) within her approach to teaching writing. She set up these discussion groups of students so that they could generate topics for writing and as a result, the classroom interaction between the students increased dramatically. The teacher realized this change in the classroom interaction: 'As the observer observed the groups working, one group at the back of the class had a lot of interaction and oral discussion and was using English'. Figure 11b shows the SCORE analysis of the communication flow in this particular group.

Often when a teacher monitors his or her own teaching, the information obtained is private and not necessarily shared with others. However, there may also be times when the information collected through self-monitoring is usefully shared with another teacher as in a critical friendship or with a group of teachers. A teaching critical friendship means engaging with another teacher 'in a way which encourages talking with, questioning, even confronting, the trusted other, in order to examine planning for teaching, implementation,

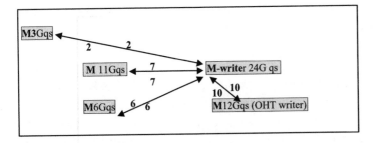

Key

M = male student
M3Gqs = male student asks 3 group questions

= asks 6 questions (top of line) and answers 6 questions (bottom of line)

Figure 11b SCORE analysis of Class 7

and its evaluation' (Hatton and Smith, 1995: 41). Peer observations within a critical friendship then is a great opportunity for teachers to develop a critically reflective stance to their own teaching. This is very important for practising teachers for as Gaies (1991: 14) has pointed out, 'What we see, when we observe teachers and learners in action, is not the mechanical application of methods and techniques, but rather a reflection of how teachers have interpreted these things'.

In order to carry out peer observations Richards and Lockhart (1994) maintain that when peers get together to observe their classes taking turns at teaching and observing, they should incorporate pre-, during and post-observation discussions. Before each observation, the teachers meet to discuss the aim of the observation and to assign the observer a goal for the observation and a task to accomplish. The teachers also agree on observation procedures or instruments (quantitative, qualitative or both) to be used during this session and arrange a schedule for the observations. During the observation, the observer then visits the teacher's class and completes the observation using the procedures that both partners had agreed on and in the post-observation discussion, the observer reports on the information that he or she collected.

In the case study reported in this chapter the teacher initiated the process and decided during the pre-observation orientation session that the observer should observe one cycle within her process approach to teaching writing. This cycle amounted to observations of seven of her classes (each class lasted two hours): the first three pre-writing activity classes, the fourth peer-response class, the fifth class which was for writing and typing the first draft of the essay and the sixth class which was for revising the first draft. The seventh class was the first class of a new cycle. For this last observation she asked the observer to 'observe any changes you see from the first cycle'. She did not ask the observer how or what to observe in any of the other classes. Thus, no specification of the role of the observer was ever made explicit. The pattern that developed was that the observer would document his observations within each phase of the cycle and only share these observations at the end of the observation cycle. Although the teacher and the observer met after each teaching session, they did not have detailed discussions about these sessions and only talked generally about the lessons. The teacher wanted to have detailed discussions after the cycle of observations was completed.

Reflection

➤ What feelings do you have associated with classroom observations?
➤ Do you feel happy that you will get feedback or worried that someone will evaluate you?
➤ What benefits would you outline for the teachers who want to experience classroom observations in their classes? What problems would you caution them against when carrying out such an exercise?
➤ Have you ever recorded (audio or video) your classroom teaching? If yes, what was your feeling? Did you find listening to (and looking at yourself) to your own voice strange? What other things did you notice?
➤ The purpose of a recording is to identify aspects of one's teaching that can only be identified through real-time recording. Discuss what aspects of a lesson can only be identified by an audio recording. Which aspects of a lesson can only be identified by a video recording?
➤ Have you ever been observed by others (apart from your students) while you were teaching? Who observed you and why? Describe your experiences of being observed.
➤ Was your experience positive or negative? If positive, what made this classroom observation experience positive? If negative, what made this classroom observation negative?
➤ What can a teacher learn from observing another teacher teach a language class?

➤ Ask a colleague to join you for classroom observations. Decide on what aspects of your teaching you would like to look at and/or discuss. Ask the friend to observe you teach and document what he/she saw. You decide what aspects of the post-observation discussion you would like to focus on. For example, you can use an adapted set of Wallace and Woolger (1991: 322) questions to answer at the end of the observations:

- Establish the facts – what did the teacher do and what did the students do?
- What was achieved? What did the students learn?
- Seeking alternatives – what else could have been done?
- Self-evaluation – what have you learned?

Conclusion

The goal of reflecting on our practice through the use of classroom observations is to become more aware of our teaching. It can also be used within peer coaching to gauge the impact of the implementation of any new practices. This becomes important for experienced language teachers because Day (1998: 268) has pointed out that most have 'already found their own personal solution to perceived problems' and do not need or want to be told what to do. However, classroom observation, either self-monitoring or with peers and groups, can help language teachers become more aware of what they do in the classroom and why they do it so that they can decide if they want to continue with such practices in the light of this new awareness. When classroom observations are handled in a non-judgemental manner where development is the goal, then they can become something teachers look forward to and which they see as time well spent rather than something to be dreaded and avoided. As Watson-Gegeo (1988: 588) says: 'By increasing their observational skills, teachers can gain new awareness of classroom organization, teaching and learning strategies, and interactional patterns in their own classrooms'.

Chapter scenario

Yoko, Hitomi and Sachiko, three female Japanese EFL teachers in different institutions in Japan, decided to meet regularly to discuss their teaching after they attended a talk on teacher development at an international language learning and teaching conference in Japan. They were especially interested in videotaping their English language classes and then watching these videotapes together in order to discuss what they observed. As they were all teaching in the Tokyo area, and within two or three subway stops, they decided that they could observe each other teach for one whole semester. However they had a few issues to discuss before the peer observations and videotaping could take place. These were:

1. Who would tape the classes? Answer: Hitomi
2. Can the observers talk to the students? Answer: No.
3. Who would act as facilitator for the discussions after the viewing? Answer: Yoko because she has the most experience teaching English (five years); Hitomi has three years' teaching experience and Yoko has two years' teaching experience.
4. Who would set the agenda for the discussions? Answer: They decided that each teacher would set the agenda when she was viewing her particular videotape of the lesson.
5. How many lessons would they observe and tape? Answer: Three for each teacher during the twelve-week semester. They also decided not to discuss each class until they had finished all three rounds of observations for all three teachers.
6. What aspects of their teaching would they focus on for discussions? Answer: As this was both their first time observing each other teach and being videotaped, and the fact that it was unusual for teachers in Japan to share their teaching and classrooms, they decided to look at general aspects of their teaching and to look for patterns in their teaching and that of the other teachers. If they discovered anything else, they could focus on that later.

After their initial nervousness of being taped, especially for Yoko as she was the most inexperienced teacher – 'The taping made me nervous. I felt I was performing for the camera' – each teacher settled down to teach her classes as she would normally do and went through the three rounds of classroom observations and videotaping smoothly. They then met to discuss the tapes and decided to devote separate meetings to discuss each set of videotapes of each teacher's class. They learned many things about their teaching as a result of the videotapes and the group discussions about their lessons.

Reflection

- What do you think of the three teachers' usage of observations?
- Look at each of the issues outlined above and discuss each issue in terms of agreement or disagreement about the outcome. Try to think of other issues a similar group may need to consider when observing, reviewing videotapes of classes and interpreting these tapes.
- Outline how each of these three teachers could develop research projects as a result of their initial findings while members of this teacher support group.
- How can classroom observations such as the ones above promote collegiality?
- How can institutions support and reward teachers who wish to carry out classroom observation on a regular basis?

12 Critical friendships

Introduction

The previous chapter on observation briefly addressed the idea of language teachers entering into critical friendships as a means of reflecting on their teaching. Developing such critical friendships may especially be important for teachers who have undergone self-monitoring (Chapter 11) of their classes and self-reflection (Chapter 2) of their practice in general because they may encounter same difficulties when confronting the self that requires such support. This support can come in the arrangement of having another teacher act as a critical friend (Stenhouse, 1975), whereby both collaborate in the exploration of teaching and learning language. This chapter discusses the process whereby language teachers can come together in critical friendships in order to reflect on their work. The discussion also includes such collaborative arrangements as team teaching and peer coaching.

What the research says

Critical friendship is a term first discussed some time ago by Stenhouse (1975) when he recommended that another person could work with a teacher and give advice as a friend rather than a consultant in order to develop the reflective abilities of the teacher who is conducting his or her own reflections. Teacher critical friendships entail entering into a collaborative arrangement with another teacher 'in a way which encourages talking with, questioning, and even confronting, the trusted other, in order to examine planning for teaching, implementation, and its evaluation' (Hatton and Smith, 1995: 41). Such critical friends can give voice to a teacher's thinking like looking into a mirror, while at the same time being heard in a sympathetic but constructively critical way. In addition, Farrell (2001b) reminds teachers that the word 'critical' in such a collaborative friendship arrangement does not, and should not connote any negativity, as the word tends to do in everyday conversation. Research has indicated that critical friendships:

- reduce the sense of isolation teachers may feel
- promote collegiality
- promote shared observation and associated benefits
- take time to evolve
- require that trust must be negotiated and earned between the teachers involved.

Team teaching is a type of critical friendship arrangement whereby two or more teachers cooperate as equals as they take responsibility for planning, teaching and evaluating a class a series of classes or a whole course (Richards and Farrell, 2005). Stewart, Sagliano and Sagliano (2002) discovered that successfully implementing a team teaching arrangement in a university in Japan where partners were equals demands a lot of time, patience and honest reflection by the teachers and administrators. In addition, Sturman (1992) noted positive outcomes of a team teaching arrangement in Japan where native and non-native teachers teamed up to teach English. Although the Japanese teachers had initially expressed low expectations about the whole idea of team teaching, as the project progressed beyond the pilot scheme, they began to feel more positive about their experiences. The native speaker teachers also had positive impressions of the team teaching experience beyond the pilot scheme as they felt that everyone gained from the experience. In addition, the students believed that their English was improving and that they had enjoyed this way of team teaching. Overall, research suggests that team teaching arrangements can have the following benefits for both teachers and institutions in which they occur:

- It provides opportunities for teachers to discuss their teaching.
- It promotes recognition and appreciation of alternative methods and techniques of teaching and evaluating lessons.
- It provides a ready-made classroom observation situation but without any evaluative component.
- It provides an effective means of teacher development.
- It provides more opportunities for individual student interaction with a teacher because there is more than one teacher in the room.

Although similar in many ways, peer coaching (another form of critical friendship) is actually different from team teaching because its main aim is for one teacher to help another improve his or her teaching. In a peer coaching arrangement there is no evaluation, no supervising, just a professional collaboration in which one teacher wants another peer to observe his/her class in order to obtain feedback on one specific aspect of teaching or learning. It focuses specifically on the process of teaching and on how two teachers can collaborate to help one or both teachers improve some aspect of their teaching. Peer coaching has the following characteristics: two teachers decide on a collaborative relationship; the two plan a series of opportunities to explore teaching collaboratively; one adopts the role of coach or 'critical friend'; they undertake a joint project or activity that involves collaborative learning; and the coach provides feedback and suggestions (Richards and Farrell, 2005). Research has indicated that peer coaching benefits language teachers because:

- It provides opportunities for teachers to look at teaching problems and to develop possible solutions.
- It is a useful way of helping beginning teachers learn from more experienced colleagues.

- It provides a supportive context in which teachers can try out new teaching strategies or methods.
- It helps develop collegiality between teachers.

Case study I: non-native speaker teacher and native speaker critical friend

The first case study presented in this chapter presents the outcome of a critical friendship where the teacher, Mee-Hee (a pseudonym), a female Korean EFL teacher wanted to reflect on her work with a critical friend (Farrell, 1999b). Mee-Hee was observed for six classes during the semester which were audio-recorded. Mee-hee also wrote a teaching journal in order to help her further reflect on her teaching. After her first class, Mee-Hee said that she was a little uncomfortable with her actual teaching methods and this was why she wanted a critical friend to observe her teach: 'I try to change my teaching method but I can't. I follow the text habitually . . . I always do that way because I learned such a way from my professor'. In reaction and after talking about this with her critical friend, Mee-Hee decided not to prescribe a book for her speech class; instead, she said she would bring in her own materials. The second class had a student standing at a podium reading a prepared speech for 35 minutes and after Mee-Hee asked all the questions until the end of class. After this class, Mee-Hee said that her lesson objective had been for the students to make a 10-minute speech followed by a question-and-answer period by the other students. When her critical friend shared his observation notes Mee-Hee commented that her class may need some change: 'I need to establish rules for the discussion and speech. Before class the speaker should give a handout of vocabulary list to the students and have time to go over the words'. She also said that she would like to know the times in the class when she asked questions and gave instructions. Both decided to use a modified version of a SCORE (Seating Chart Observation Record) chart (see Chapter 11) because Mee-Hee was familiar with this instrument. Figure 12a outlines the SCORE analysis after Mee-Hee's third class.

The SCORE shows a lot of back-and-forth flow of communication between the speaker and the students (after the speech) in the form of questions and answers. Mee-Hee was surprised to find out from this SCORE analysis that

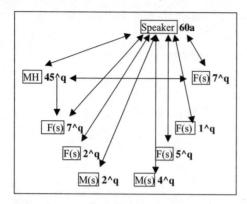

Figure 12a SCORE analysis of Mee-Hee's third class
Key: F(s) = female student; M(s) = male student; MH = Mee-Hee (the teacher); q = ask; a = answer question. The long arrows show the directional flow of the questions and answers.

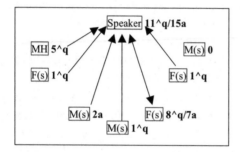

Figure 12b SCORE analysis of Mee-Hee's fourth class
Key: F(s) = female student; M(s) = male student; MH = Mee-Hee (the teacher); q = ask; a = answer question. The long arrows show the directional flow of the questions and answers.

she had asked 45 questions during the class as she said she had thought that she was 'a silent participant as a listener in my classes'. She continued, 'Until now I had no realization about my questioning pattern'. She decided to change these patterns. The SCORE analysis of Mee-Hee's fourth class is shown in Figure 12b.

This SCORE analysis shows a dramatic change in the communication pattern. The critical friend's observation notes showed that at the beginning of the class when the speaker and the other students realized that Mee-Hee was going to stay silent they got on with the class themselves and the discussion after the presentation even included a sustained competitive discussion between one female student (on the right of the SCORE analysis figure) and the speaker.

Case study I reflection

➤ Discuss what you think of the critical friendship process as outlined in the case study above.
➤ What was the role of the critical friend in this case study?
➤ Why do you think Mee-Hee was able to look at her classroom practice more critically and move beyond descriptions of what she was doing?
➤ How do you gauge how many questions you ask in class?
➤ Mee-Hee says that she wants to personalize topics to Korean culture. What do you think about personalizing topics that are in the textbook?

Case study II: native speaker teacher and native speaker critical friend

The second case study presented in this chapter concerns another example of a critical friendship which lasted over a period of 16 weeks. An Australian English as a foreign language (EFL) teacher in Korea and a native speaker critical friend (this author) came together, to consider the professional development of both participants. This example will focus only on the reflections of the EFL teacher in the critical friendship dyad and report the results. The initial goal of the critical friendship was to talk about teaching in general and the teaching of a set of specific classes in a private company in particular and all at the teacher's request. The teacher also kept a teaching journal and wrote whenever he wanted to. The teacher, Greg, was teaching an English conversation class which was part of a private company's ongoing education programme. The objective of the course was to increase the students' (who were all company employees) English conversational ability.

Greg invited the critical friend to visit his classes and observe with the use of a video camera (both negotiated this and agreed it would be good for the reflection process.) No specific role was discussed for the critical friend except to manage the observation process of his teaching and to try to stimulate discussion of the teacher's teaching after observed classes. The discussions after each observed lesson usually started with the teacher evaluating his lesson either positively or negatively. He then tried to interpret the students' interactions and/or problems he perceived that they had encountered. For example, in one meeting, he started with a negative evaluation of his lesson. He said that he was disappointed with the class. He continued:

> I must work harder on the lead in to my introduction, but still I am unsatisfied, I had wanted them to talk more. I was not happy with Y.S., speaking a lot of Korean. A good lesson for me is when students are talking together; today they were not talking, so it was not a good lesson.

On one later occasion he asked the critical friend for suggestions on how to check what his students had learned in each class. The critical friend suggested he use a short questionnaire that he had used in his own classes that asked four short questions as follows:

1. What do you think you learned today?
2. What was easy for you?
3. What was difficult for you and why?
4. What did you enjoy?

He decided to use the questionnaire at the end of his following class near the end of the reflection process. In his teaching journal he wrote that the students gave less than flattering answers: 'Two [out of a class of seven] did not understand the first question, and one answered he did not enjoy anything, and said nothing was interesting'. Even though he was surprised by these answers, the process of asking his students for their perceptions caused him to reflect on his teaching in general; 'I haven't looked at my teaching. I haven't been looking at my class and my teaching closely, only vague and theoretical'. As a result in the final discussion he said he would try to change: 'I am trying to develop a new teaching method because I don't want to continue the same old way. I have to work harder'.

Case study II reflection

➤ Discuss what you think of the critical friendship process as outlined in the case study above.
➤ What was the role of the critical friend in case study II?
➤ The teacher in case study II above said that he would follow his lesson plan even if the class was not going well. What is your opinion of this?

➤ The teacher also said that he judges the success of the class by how the students react. What is your opinion of this?
➤ What is your opinion of the short questionnaire that the critical friend gave to Greg?
➤ How do you judge if your teaching is successful?

From research to practice

Critical friends

Critical friends are teachers who collaborate in a two-way mode that encourages discussion and reflection in order to improve the quality of language teaching and learning. This collaboration incorporates Schrange's (1990: 40) depiction of collaboration as 'the process of shared creation' wherein 'two or more individuals with complementary skills [interact] to create a shared understanding that none had previously possessed or could have come to on their own'. This type of collaboration requires teachers to embark on reflection; however, not all teachers are ready to reflect (Moon and Boullon 1997). Therefore, the readiness of the teacher should be considered before the process begins. Since critical friendship means self-disclosure and some process of change, the person who is reflecting should be in a good personal psychological state in order to be able to confront any inconsistencies that may occur. It should be understood that reflection can cause doubt, and that for this reason some people may not want to face any further uncertainties at this stage of their life.

That said, it may also be necessary within the friendship when trust has been established that the friend not be afraid of challenging the teacher if he or she observes instances where the teacher could be challenged. As Hatton and Smith (1995) suggest this challenging by the critical friend may be very necessary for a deeper examination and evaluation of teaching. In case study II outlined in this chapter the teacher said that he judged successful teaching on his students' reactions (or lack of reactions) and when they exhibited any signs of boredom (such as yawning or glazed eyes) he evaluated these signs of distress or non-involvement as his inability to entertain the students; he commented:

> It is a reflection on you if they are not involved. I must entertain them. If they are not involved, it is a reflection on you as you are not popular and we must get more people to come. I am interested in attention getting; there is no learning if there is no interest. Entertainment is a performance, not like music, like theater. I must get more interesting topics.

When challenged by the critical friend that he may want to consider changing his lesson plan, Greg was not convinced as he said he would 'stick to the lesson plan even if it wasn't going well'. In a later discussion he said that he was still concerned with his students' silence and he became very sensitive to their reactions in his class. The critical friend challenged him again to not look at each specific reaction and Greg agreed that 'Maybe I am too sensitive but a slight indication of tiredness, yawning or eyes not focused or not looking at the book is a sign of distress' for him. He said he would work at reconciling this. When challenged about his theories of teaching, he said that he was somewhat confused. He continued:

> I do not really know what I am doing. I do not plan in advance; it is not that I am not organized; it is a problem of knowledge about teaching. Sometimes I am grasping at straws. I want to fill up the time. Now I want to get down to work and leave theory behind. It is necessary to go further in ESL, but I do not know how.

As it turned out, he started a Master's degree in Education around the same time and possibly as a way to look deeper into his teaching. Even though the critical friendship did not produce any observable change in the teacher's teaching behaviours, it was, nevertheless, successful in providing him with a forum to begin probing his teaching theories and beliefs; he seemed comfortable when talking with me after his class, although these discussions were general in nature. In his journal he wrote: 'Conversation with the critical friend after class was a meeting of the minds. We were on the same wavelength and it was possible to say what I thought and I felt good after it'. Similarly, in case study I outlined in this chapter Mee-Hee's reflections six months after her experiences with the critical friend were mostly positive. Although she said it was difficult for her to look at her own teaching, she nevertheless said that she is now 'a more empowered teacher'. As Francis (1995) says, 'Critical friends can stimulate, clarify, and extend thinking . . . and feel accountable for their own growth and their peers' (p. 234).

Team teaching

In language teaching critical friendships can be formed as a stand-alone general reflective arrangement outlined above, or in a more focused team teaching or peer coaching arrangement. Teachers who come together to team-teach a course (or a lesson) must first consider what roles each will play within the team so that they can collaborate successfully. Richards and Farrell (2005) outline some of the following team teaching arrangements that teams can choose from depending on what best meets their needs:

- *Equal partners*: both teachers see themselves as having an equal experience and knowledge and so all decisions are shared equally for all stages of the lesson: planning, delivery, monitoring and checking.
- *Leader and participant*: one teacher is given or assumes a leadership role because he or she has more experience with team teaching.
- *Mentor and apprentice*: one teacher is recognized as an expert teacher (and thus takes more responsibility) while the other is a novice.
- *Native/advanced speaker and less-proficient speaker*: in some situations (such as in Japan's JET programme and Korea's KET programme) a native English language speaker or an advanced speaker of English may team-teach with a less proficient speaker. In some cases the native/ advanced speaker takes responsibility for those aspects of the lesson that are more linguistically demanding but in many cases the lesson takes place in the less proficient speaker's class so he or she must take responsibility for setting up the lesson.

Next, teams should realize that team teaching is just that, a team, not two individuals', approach to planning the lessons, deciding and preparing the activities, delivering the lessons, and evaluating the effectiveness of the lessons. Both members of the team should take equal responsibility for every stage of the teaching process and trust each other throughout. Of course, team teaching must also allow for teachers who have differing personalities, teaching styles and even planning styles. In order to accommodate such differences, Struman (1992: 169) suggests that the team consider 'the principle of flexible equality' whereby teachers with different personalities acknowledge these differences and not to try to avoid or bury them. Instead, the teachers can define their roles and responsibilities that are most suitable for their own individual needs and situations. Teachers in a team teaching arrangement must then decide more specific day-to-day actions that take into account such logistical issues as who will begin each class and who will finish the class if they decide both will teach each class. Alternatively, the team can decide that one teacher will teach (and possibly plan) one complete class. If this is the case, then the team must decide what the other teacher's role will be (and where the other teacher will sit or stand and if the teacher will join in or not). One useful exercise here would be for the team to ask the students in each class what they would prefer in such arrangements because they are supposed to be the ultimate beneficiaries of a team teaching arrangement. The best of all worlds here would be a combination of all that has been discussed above at least for the first few classes so that both the team and the students can decide which arrangement best suits teaching and learning needs.

If team teaching is adopted by the administration of a school as is sometimes the case, Richards and Farrell (2005) suggest that it is very important that each team knows what the overall aim of the team teaching programme is because team teaching may not be for everybody. It is important then for the administration to inform their teachers about certain aspects of team teaching such as:

- if it is voluntary
- if one gets to choose who to teach with or not
- how much time it will take
- the amount of extra work it will involve
- how conflict between teachers in a team will be resolved
- how the students will be briefed about the team teaching process
- how the teams will be evaluated

Stewart, Sagliano and Sagliano (2002) outline an interesting institutionally arranged team teaching situation in which prior to each term the teachers choose partners by making a ranked selection of desired co-teachers. Administrators then set the teams by matching first and second choices. Each teaching pair negotiates their own procedures for developing and teaching a course. Then as equal partners, co-teachers jointly create materials, teach simultaneously in the classroom, and determine grades. The authors concluded that successful implementation of team teaching demands time, patience, honest reflection, by both teachers and the administration.

Peer coaching

A peer coaching arrangement takes place so that the observed teacher can develop new knowledge and skills and a deeper awarness of his/her own teaching. To make the peer coaching work successfully, each participant must recognize that he or she has a specific role to follow in the peer coaching relationship. For example, peer coaches can help their less experienced teachers in the following general ways (adapted from Bova and Phillips, 1981):

- To encourage less experienced teachers in setting and attaining short- and long-term goals.
- To teach less experienced teachers the skills necessary to survive and promote career-scope professional development.
- To protect less experienced teachers by limiting their exposure to responsibility.
- To provide opportunities for less experienced teachers to observe and participate in their work.
- To act as role models.

In addition, Gottesman (2000: 37) suggests the following roles for the teacher in a peer coaching relationship:

- Be committed to peer coaching to analyse and improve instruction.
- Be willing to develop and use a common language of collaboration in order to discuss the total teaching act without praise or blame.
- To request to enter into a peer coaching relationship (e.g., by requesting a classroom observation visit and to observe as a coach if so asked).
- Be open-minded and willing to look for better ways of conducting classroom business.
- Act as a colleague and as a professional.

Classroom observations can be phased into peer coaching in a typical developmental classroom observation four-step sequence of pre-observation discussion, actual classroom visit, post-visit discussion and general review of the process. The teacher can take the first step in a peer coaching situation by requesting a visit from a more experienced or knowledgeable peer to come to his/her class for a limited period of time. At this pre-observation stage both the teacher and the peer coach should attempt to establish common ground rules about the process during this phase so that there is no misunderstanding. For example, the teacher and the coach should agree what kind of feedback will be given to the teacher after the classroom visit. The teacher then teaches a class where a peer coach is also present but does not get involved in any way. The classroom visit may be audiorecorded and/or videorecorded depending on the issue of investigation and a lesson transcript may also be prepared for later discussions if both teacher and coach think it useful for their purposes. The two teachers later meet and discuss what was written and what was achieved. This discussion initially focuses on the information that the coach collected as was agreed to in the pre-observation meeting. After the information has been shared, the teacher can ask the peer coach to make specific suggestions for further development of the issue under scrutiny and they can enter into another cycle of observation after this to see if the new suggestions have had an impact on the teacher's teaching. Teacher and coach can then review the whole process especially if they want to switch roles – the teacher becomes the coach for his/her fellow teacher.

Reflection

➤ Have you ever experienced a critical friendship relationship? If yes, describe your experiences.
➤ What is your understanding of the term 'critical' in critical friendship relationships?
➤ When teachers meet as critical friends, they should focus more on the friend and less on the critical. Discuss this approach to critical friendship.
➤ Have you ever experienced a team teaching relationship? If yes, describe your experiences.
➤ How was the relationship set up, and what were the different roles played by each team member?
➤ Do you think it is possible for two teachers to take equal responsibility for planning and teaching a class? If not, why not?
➤ How can the students benefit from having two teachers teach the same lesson?
➤ Both teachers in a team teaching relationship have certain roles to play. Discuss these different roles and outline possible problems that may arise within each role.
➤ How can peer coaching benefit the teacher, the coach and the school?
➤ Richards and Farrell (2005) suggest that feedback in a peer coaching relationship should take the form of 'No Praise, No Blame'. What is your understanding of this?
➤ The peer coach has a specific role to play in a peer coaching relationship. Discuss this role and outline possible problems that may arise between the teacher and the coach.

Conclusion

This chapter outlined three different arrangements in which language teachers can collaborate to reflect on their teaching. The three collaborative arrangements are critical friendships, peer coaching and team teaching. The main idea of entering a critical friendship is that two (or more) teachers can gain from having a trusted other comment on their teaching in a non-judgemental manner. The main purposes of peer coaching is to support a teacher's existing strengths rather than to evaluate him/her. Peer coaching can help inexperienced teachers learn from more experienced colleagues in a supportive environment so that they try out new teaching methods and get feedback. In a team teaching arrangement usually two teachers equally share the responsibility for teaching and evaluating a class so that each teacher can learn more about the strengths and expertise of their colleague. All three collaborative arrangements follow Robbins' (1991: 1) ideas of colleagues working together 'to reflect on current practices, expand, refine, and build new skills, share ideas; teach one another; conduct classroom research; or solve problems in the workplace'.

Chapter scenario

Anna and Carmen are both American teachers teaching in a private institute in Taiwan. They each teach four classes but team-teach one of them. For that class, they plan the class together. They divide up the activities in each unit of their textbook deciding who will teach which exercises and which exercises they will present together. They plan each of their lessons to determine their roles within the lesson. They are both present for every lesson and share the teaching time. They both enjoy their team-taught lessons and feel that both they and their learners benefit from them. The following example shows how Anna and Carmen planned an intermediate level reading class:

Lesson objectives:
- To teach the students to skim to find the main idea of a passage
Prior knowledge:
- Students have learned how to locate information by reading and finding the main sentence of each paragraph. This lesson is to practise increasing their reading speed within scanning and skimming for information.

Materials:

- Reading materials – a passage from their textbook on sports plus supplementary materials
- Overhead projector

Lesson plan:

- **Stage I**: Opening (5–10 minutes): Introduction to the topic – sport. Anna activates students' background knowledge on sports and asks students to suggest as many different kinds of sport within 3 minutes. Anna asks students to rank their favourite sports in order of importance. As the students call out their answers Carmen writes them on the board.
- **Stage II**: Anna distributes handout on sports schedule from the newspaper and worksheet. Carmen asks the students to read it quickly and answer the true/false questions about it within 3 minutes. Carmen goes over the answers. At this stage of the lesson Carmen wants to focus on the concept of skimming for general gist with authentic materials.
- **Stage III**: Carmen discusses skimming to get the general meaning or gist of a passage. Anna asks students to turn to a text on sport in the textbook. Anna asks the students to read and answer the true/false questions within 5–7 minutes. Anna asks students for answers and writes them on the board.
- **Stage IV**: Closing: Carmen summarizes the importance of reading a passage quickly first in order to get the gist. Carmen gives homework of reading the next day's newspaper front page story and writing down in four sentences the gist of the story.
- **Follow-up**: Carmen and Anna meet briefly after class in order to evaluate the lesson they just taught.

Post-lesson discussion

- Carmen and Anna discussed their lesson in the staffroom immediately after class. They decided to look at what they thought went well and what they were unsure about. Both were pleased at the way the students were able to follow their instructions and directions. Anna, however felt that Carmen's instructions for the skimming phase of the lesson were a bit fast as some of the students near her did not do what was required of them until they asked Anna for clarification. Carmen had not realized this. They also realized that the changeover from Carmen to Anna to use the text in stage III did not go smoothly. So they decided to make two changes for the next team teaching session:

(1) To back up oral instructions with written instructions on the whiteboard in future so there would be fewer misunderstandings. (2) Decide on one of them to take responsibility for each stage with the other teacher acting as a resource person like distributing handouts, or writing answers on the board (as happened in stage II). This way, they hoped the students would not become confused about who was teaching them and who to answer when asked questions. Overall, though, they were very pleased that way the lesson went and looked forward to the next session.

Reflection

- What do you think about this team teaching arrangement?
- Think up a different possible post-lesson discussion between Anna and Carmen.
- Try to experience a similar critical friendship and/or a team teaching arrangement and/or a peer coaching arrangement with colleagues in your school or district.
- How can a school/institution best support a critical friendship arrangement in a school?
- How can a school/institution best support a peer coaching arrangement and/or programme in a school?
- How can a school/institution best support a team teaching arrangement and/or programme in a school?
- What would be the main concerns of the teachers in a school where a team teaching and or peer coaching programme was implemented by the administration?
- How can the administration best address these concerns?

13 Concept mapping

Introduction

Concept maps are 'a visual representation of knowledge' (Antonacci, 1991: 174) and show relationships among concepts within a specific field of knowledge (Novak, 1990). Concept maps show relationships between concepts in a type of network where any concept or idea can be connected to any other and as such are a useful indication of what people know about a topic. The technique of concept mapping, originally from the field of cognitive psychology, has now been used by both teachers and students as a means of reflecting on teaching and learning. This chapter outlines and discusses how the technique of concept mapping can be a very effective tool to assist second language teachers reflect on their teaching.

What the research says

Concept mapping has been defined by Meijer, Verloop and Beijaard (1999) as a 'technique for capturing and graphically representing concepts and their hierarchical interrelationships' (p. 62). For language educators according to Mergendoller and Sachs (1994: 589), concept mapping can be 'useful for measuring cognitive change resulting from participation in academic courses'. In addition, for students wishing to reflect on their learning, Van Bruggen, Kirschner and Jochems (2002) have suggested that concept mapping can be a very effective way to relate new concepts to a person's current knowledge and can encourage more involvement in their own learning process. This reflective learning occurs because the concept mapping activity helps both teachers and students communicate what (and how) they are thinking through visual patterns of thinking. Fischer, Bruhn, Grasel and Mandl (2002) suggest that students construct their own concept maps, rather than have a pre-course map prepared by the course instructor, to ensure greater ownership of the learning process. Research on concept mapping suggests that:

- It contributes to ownership in the learning process.
- It provides a means of teacher reflection.
- It provides a means of student reflection.
- It helps students relate current knowledge to new knowledge.
- It gives an overall picture of the learning process.
- It provides teachers with information about students' levels of learning.

Case study: 'What did they really learn?'

The following case study reports on how concept mapping was used to gauge what students learned as a result of taking a TESOL Reading Methods course (Farrell, 2006d). The course consisted of nine classes (18 hours of class time over 9 weeks) of instruction on reading theory, teaching strategies and current concepts. The course emphasized the following concepts in current reading theory: schema theory, the role of prior knowledge, psycholinguistic theory and reading, metacognition and self-monitoring techniques, text structure, techniques to promote the use of effective reading strategies, vocabulary teaching, and actual lesson plan writing and critiquing.

On the first day of class, 20 students were asked to construct a concept map of the reading process and the teaching of English reading. The first maps created were for diagnostic purposes; to give the instructor an

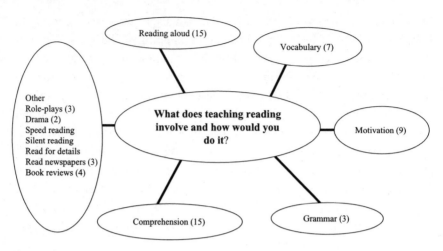

Figure 13a Pre-course group concept map showing frequency of topics
Key: Number in parentheses shows how many teachers included that topic in their concept maps.

indication of the students' beliefs about their prior knowledge. They all received the same written (and orally explained) directions, together with an example of a concept map. At the start of the following class, the instructor presented a pre-course group concept map drawn from all the individual maps (see Figure 13a).

Figure 13a illustrates that the group had no shared understanding of what it means to teach reading. On the final day of class, the teachers were again asked to construct individual concept maps showing their understanding of the reading process and teaching reading. When class members completed their post-course maps, their individual pre-course maps were returned for comparison. They were asked to write comments about any changes they noticed and the reasons for these changes. Figure 13b shows the post-course group concept map constructed from these individual maps.

Overall, the post-course group concept map was more extensive and more complex than the pre-course group concept map. The new topics in the post-course map included extensive reading, teach reading strategies, text awareness, lesson planning and metacognition awareness. During random interviews with some of the students it was discovered that talking to the teachers about their maps was an important addition to this technique because many students became more aware not only of their own conceptions of teaching reading but also of some knowledge gaps and inconsistencies in their construction of the post-course concept maps.

Figure 13b Post-course group concept map showing frequency of topics
Key: Number in parentheses shows how many teachers included that topic in their concept maps.

Case study reflection

➤ One important reason for undertaking this case study was to find out if the course had any impact on the learner teachers. Do you think the course had any impact based on the differences between the two maps? If yes, why? If not, why not?

➤ Do you think that local culture can have any impact on the way our students respond to such concept maps? Explain.

➤ How do you think concept mapping could help you as a language teacher reflect and at the same time your students reflect on their learning?

➤ How do you think the interviews may have enabled the students to critically reflect on the concepts they used?

➤ Construct your own concept map about how to teach each skill such as reading, writing, speaking, listening and grammar and compare your inclusion and exclusion of concepts with what you find in various methodology books.

From research to practice

Concept maps can be used by both teachers and students to reflect on their teaching and learning. Concept maps can be used as a type of meta-language by teachers to document and analyse their beliefs and by students to describe their learning. They can be used not only for communication but also synthesizing what a teacher is thinking and a student is learning. They can also be used to show how the learner is thinking about course content, and teachers can use them to evaluate what students know and more importantly *how* they know what they know. Concept mapping can be used by individual language teachers and by facilitators of language teacher development courses. They can be used by individual language teachers to gauge their personal understandings of a particular topic because concept maps help provide a visual means of how they store words and ideas about a topic until they decide what to do with them.

Language teachers can use concept maps with their second language students, for example, at the beginning of a new lesson in order to gauge how much their students have learned from previous lessons and/or to discuss any misunderstandings that may have occurred about the content of previous lessons. Zaid (1995) has maintained that teachers can use concept mapping within a lesson in three places: as pre-activity for diagnostic purposes for the teacher and/or as a way to get students ready for a particular topic. They can also have students use concept maps during lessons as a record of what they are learning and teachers can later look at these maps to see if both are on the same track. Finally, teachers can use concept maps as a post-assignment in lessons to see how their students understood concepts presented in the lessons. Of course, students also benefit from this type of reflection as they can see (literally) what they know before, during and after the lesson. In order to implement a concept mapping activity, Zaid (1995) has suggested several useful procedures for using concept maps in classes three of which are.

- *Introduce topic.* The teacher introduces the topic by drawing (on whatever surface the teacher usually uses in his or her classroom) a large oval and placing the topic inside that oval. Next, the teacher draws several nodes, or spokes that move straight from that oval like a bicycle wheel.
- *Brainstorm topic.* The teacher then asks students to generate ideas about the topic within the oval and writes whatever responses related to the topic they tell him at the end of each spoke that come from the oval.
- *Categorization:* Next the teacher attempts to get the students to make links between all the responses and as a result forms "category clusters" (Antonacci, 1991: 174) and puts these within ovals, one oval for each category related to the central topic. These ovals are said to exist at a secondary level and of course can proceed down to other levels depending on the amount of detail provided. If students have any difficulties identifying categories, they can be asked Wh-questions (Who, What, When, Where, How) as prompts.

This can be accomplished through the use of individual student concept maps or have students work collaboratively in pairs or groups to complete a concept map. Teachers can also compile a class group concept map from these individual maps, as was utilized in the case study reported on in this chapter. When educators use concept maps they can change the manner of discourse in the class as they change the way they talk to their students as they use words such as *think, classify, sequence, brainstorm* and *reflect* and in turn students can actually *use* these words which also represent cognitive processes. Thus concept maps help language educators teach cognitive processes to students as well as course content as these words of reflection are woven through ongoing conversations about the students' understanding of concepts provided during the course. In addition, educators should realize that learning is individual and that individual students internalize information presented in courses in different ways and that concept mapping supports internal dialogue as they mediate thinking between students and teacher. For educators pre-course concept maps encourage them to identify the goals and purposes of a course and each lesson before actual instruction and as such they can determine what kind of thinking will be involved throughout the course. Similarly for students, before they begin a lesson they can, by looking at their concept maps, especially if they construct a concept map for each lesson, ask themselves what learning and thinking may be necessary for completion of the lesson.

When used in a teacher development course, concept mapping can provide an impetus for teachers to begin to consider alternatives about what they hold to be true about a topic as they can change the way teachers talk to each other as they use the language of their map. In order to use concept mapping effectively for teachers to develop their self-understanding of their knowledge, facilitators of a teacher development course should first provide a *sample concept map* because this technique may not be familiar to all teachers and they will thus benefit from an illustration of what is expected. While providing an example of the concept map, the facilitator can model reflective thinking of such a map by *thinking aloud* about the construction of the map as the facilitator puts his or her concepts of a particular topic as represented on a visual concept map into verbal thought. The preparation of clear written instructions is also essential at this stage to ensure that all respondents have a comparable understanding of the task they are being asked to complete; if this is not the case (e.g. if vague instructions mean that teachers interpret the requirements of the task in different ways) conclusions based on comparisons across teachers will be questionable. One idea to make instructions clear is to include some kind of *brainstorming* of the topic in focus to generate a preliminary list of related concepts and then this can be followed by creating a diagram (concept map) which shows the participants' understanding of how these and more concepts they want to add are related. During the brainstorming sessions it is important to encourage that all ideas are welcome and acceptable but that they must be provided within a given time frame. The final stage is the actual construction of the concept map.

One of the findings of the case study reported on in this chapter was that it may be important to have an opportunity to talk about the contents of the concept map the teacher constructs. Novak and Gowin (1984) maintain that because concept maps are an externalization of what teachers think, they may not always be a reliable guide to this thinking, so it is difficult to judge how accurate the representation is. For example, during the interviews conducted during the case study outlined above, the maps allowed the teachers to see what they were thinking and made it easier for them to retrieve language to express that knowledge in a clear and organized way. This may be very important for second language teachers and students who thus far may have struggled to find a voice to express their knowledge of a particular topic and may have decided to remain silent rather than to suffer the pain and frustration of expressing their thoughts. As a result of explaining their own conceptions, the participants in the case study reported that they have gained a greater conceptual clarity for themselves. This is a major prerequisite for change, because by becoming aware of one's own conceptions, knowledge gaps and inconsistent reasoning can be considered as important conditions for conceptual change, because they may have resulted in a type of cognitive conflict.

Reflection

➢ How might construction of a concept map on a particular topic aid you in your teacher reflections?
➢ What difficulties do you foresee when attempting to construct concept maps?
➢ How can these difficulties be overcome?
➢ Do your students reflect on their learning regularly? If so, how? If not, why not?
➢ Why is it a good idea for teachers to get their students to reflect on their learning?
➢ How do you think concept maps can measure conceptual change as a result of taking a particular course of study?
➢ When educators use concept maps they can change the manner of discourse in the class as they change the way they talk to their students as they use words such as *think, classify, sequence, brainstorm* and *reflect* and in turn students can actually *use* these words which also represent cognitive processes. Explain how you think this process may work.
➢ Brainstorm a topic for reflection with a group of other language teachers and then construct concept maps about that topic. Compare your concept maps and explain each individually. What did you learn from this process?

Conclusion

Concept mapping allows language teachers to have a visual format of the concepts they 'see' as being important for a particular topic. As a result, teachers can reflect on their meaning and how these maps represent their underlying beliefs about the topic in focus. Teachers can also use concept mapping in their course to gauge current knowledge about concepts under discussion and in order to trace the participants' conceptual change as a result of taking the course. In this way, both teacher and student are forced to reflect on the content of a course as both engage in evaluative reflection.

Chapter scenario

Although concept mapping may seem to be a complex and time-consuming way to look at cognitive changes in teacher thinking, I have used concept mapping to stimulate teachers' reflections even when there was no prepared list of concepts. With this approach, teachers were asked to generate concepts relating to a topic and they have reported that it can facilitate their reflections on their beliefs and knowledge about a particular topic. Recently I have used this technique of concept mapping in my MA courses in Canada and can report that concept mapping (pre-course and post-course) is useful because it encourages both the teacher and students to reflect before, during and after the course. In the context of my courses in Canada, I asked teachers who were taking a Foundations in Applied Linguistics and TESL course to construct concept maps about their understanding of TESOL and Applied Linguistics so they could then become more aware of their understanding of the course material before and after the course and thus take more charge of their own meaning-making about the field of Applied Linguistics. Pre-course and post-course concept maps were elicited from the teachers who were also asked to write short descriptions of changes (and the reasons for these changes) they observed between their pre- and post-course maps. All participants were also interviewed about the contents of their individual concept maps. Preliminary results indicate that the course had some impact on the teachers' prior beliefs and experience about Applied Linguistics and TESL and especially in fostering a new sense of critical reflection about the profession. The teachers all wrote that they noticed a major new concept present in their post-course maps that was not present in the pre-course maps, that of critical reflection. For example, in his post-course reflection one Canadian teacher realized that he just accepted all he was presented with even when he was taking his TESL Certificate at a different university some years previous; he continues:

> There were moments, in my teaching profession, until now, where I've done something 'cause that's the way I've done it. And, if someone asked me, I would say 'well, this is – this is, like, the way to do it because it's effective'. But without really questioning the context that I was in and not . . . Without really questioning what was going on.

Another interesting strong pattern that emerged in the post-course maps was a different understanding of the concept 'method' as the participants noted that they now tended to move away from a focus on looking for the correct method as they did when constructing the pre-course concept maps. For instance, one teacher from Asia said that she now realizes 'that there is no correct method'. So for me, concept mapping was a quick and efficient way of gauging the extent of the impact of my course on these graduate students. I agree with Novak and Gowin (1984: 40) that the maps did not give a complete picture, but they did provide a 'workable approximation' and when backed up by interviews, they can as Wilson (1998: 8) maintains, 'promote class discussion, correction of student misconceptions, and learning and retention of complex concepts and principles'.

Reflection

- Now might be a good time for you to construct a concept map which has as its central concept place within the oval: 'What does Teaching English as a second/foreign/subsequent language mean to you?' Draw several nodes or spokes coming from the centre oval and see if you can make category clusters.
- How many secondary categories were you able to construct?
- What difficulties did you have (if any) when constructing this map?
- What information does this map tell you about your knowledge of this general question?
- If you do this activity with other teachers, compare your concept maps and discuss the contents of each map.
- Did you uncover any misconceptions about the topic as a result of discussions and comparisons with other teachers?

Professional development through reflective language teaching

14

Introduction

The need for ongoing teacher development has been a recent recurring theme in the field of second language teaching, not a reflection of inadequately trained teachers but a response to the fact that not everything a language teacher needs to know can be provided at pre-service level, and also that the knowledge base of teaching is constantly changing (Richards and Farrell,

2005). This chapter outlines and discusses how second language teachers engage in self-renewal and professional development through reflective language teaching.

What the research says

Research suggests that teachers who are better informed about their teaching are also better able to evaluate what aspects of their practice they may need to adjust because they are more aware of what stage they have reached in their professional development (Richards and Lockhart, 1994). Professional development for second language teachers, defined as the 'process of continual intellectual, experiential, and attitudinal growth of teachers' (Lange, 1990: 250), has more often than not, consisted of district or administration mandated courses and one-stop workshops conducted by outside 'experts' in a top-down approach to the dissemination of knowledge in which teachers are subsequently expected to translate into action in order to improve their practice (Clair, 1998). While suggestions for improving practice with such a top-down delivered system may be well intentioned, its real impact is limited because teachers may find that many of the ideas presented are often conceptually and practically far removed from the reality of their particular classrooms. In fact, throughout their careers, many second language teachers have been expected to learn about their own profession by studying the findings of outside experts, but not by studying their own experiences. Johnson and Golombek (2002: 3), however, have recently called for a new approach within second language education that recognizes teachers as 'legitimate knowers, producers of legitimate knowledge, and as capable of constructing and sustaining their own professional practice over time'. In addition, and as the contents of this book suggest, much can be learned about teaching through self-inquiry rather than drawing solely on experts' opinions or theories.

One of the key themes, as was mentioned in Chapter 1, of second language teacher development research recently is that it is a process of articulating an inner world of choices 'made in response to the outer world of the teaching context' (Mann, 2005: 105). Mann (2005) has further proposed that detailed accounts are needed about experienced language teachers' existing beliefs, assumptions, values and knowledge concerning their work so that we can acknowledge this personal conceptualization within the knowledge-base of second language teacher education. This bottom-up approach to reflection starts from the assumption that teachers, not methods or expert opinions, make a difference as they explore the nature of their own decision-making and classroom practices. Bottom-up professional development of this kind can be accomplished when language teachers collect information about their practice, either alone or in collaboration with other colleagues, and where a 'good' teacher is seen as one who accesses the needs and possibilities of his or her particular context and teaching situation. That said, Rose (2006: 67) has noted that the exact pattern of each teacher's development will be different and unique in that 'some teachers develop quickly, others more slowly'. Rose (2006) also suggests that teachers identify a range of different catalysts that lead them to a change in behaviour and likens professional development of language teachers to a journey which starts with inexperience, then undergoes further study until the teacher gets the feeling of having arrived as a professional. The arrival phase is characterized by a recognition that they themselves must be able to judge their own teaching because they may not have opportunities of being observed and so must be able to monitor their own teaching regularly.

Research has also shown that many experienced teachers have been routinely applying classroom strategies without much reflection, and although experience as a teacher may be a good starting point for development, it is necessary to examine such experience systematically in order to learn from it (Richards and Lockhart, 1994). Wajnryb (1992: 9) also links reflective practice to professional development in that she considers reflective language teachers those who are 'discovering more about their own teaching by seeking to understand the processes of teaching and learning in their own and others' classrooms'. As mentioned in Chapter 1, Hoover (1994) noted that although the concept of reflective teaching has been seen as promising to many educators over the years, he also pointed out that little research had been conducted as to its validity. In the past 15 years the results of my own research (much of it outlined in this book) and research conducted by other second language educators now suggest that language teachers who engage in reflective language teaching can develop the following:

- a deeper understanding of teaching
- an evaluation of what stage they are at in their professional growth
- more skills in self-reflection and critical thinking
- more complex and clearer schema about teaching
- a more coherent personal approach to classroom teaching
- more elaborate pedagogical reasoning skills
- more informed decision-making skills
- more proactive and confident teachers

Case study: tailoring reflection to individual needs

The case study reports on the reflections of one non-native English speaker Korean teacher (Heesoon, a pseudonym) of English as a foreign language (EFL) in Korea and her preferred mode of reflection among three different types: group talking, classroom observations and journal writing (Farrell, 2001a). Heesoon said that she joined the group because she was seeking to become a better teacher. She continued: 'I must also be able to find myself as a teacher by systematically looking at what I already know and do, examining all the ideas presented and then answering [Heeson's] own problems on the basis of [my] own experience'.

Throughout all the group meetings Heesoon was a very active participant. She tried to get involved in many of the discussions that the other members had initiated and was always non-judgemental in her comments. During the group discussions, Heesoon was interested in talking about her personal theories of teaching and her students' level of motivation. Also, Heesoon talked a lot about her students' level of motivation. However, Heesoon did not show the same level of participation in the other two modes of reflection: classroom observations and journal writing. In fact, Heesoon stopped after two classroom observations because she said that she was not ready for 'that level of scrutiny by an outsider'.

Heesoon used her teaching journal infrequently for reflection. Out of a total of six entries, she wrote mostly about her class procedures. Heesoon said that she did not feel comfortable writing about her teaching; she felt that she could not achieve reflection through the medium of writing. At the last group meeting, she revealed the extent of her lack of enthusiasm for writing: 'I always felt that I had to write something down, but I didn't have anything to write'. So Heesoon considered writing a teaching journal a difficult task. However, during the group discussions Heesoon found support offered by the other members of the group that she said was missing in the 'lonely work of having to write about teaching'. The conclusion of this case study is that reflection should be tailored to an individual teacher's needs and preferences.

Case study reflection

➤ In the above case study, Heesoon said she was comfortable in a group situation talking with other teachers. Why do you think she liked to talk with other teachers about her teaching?

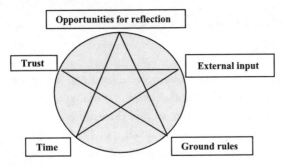

Figure 14 Framework for reflective language teaching

➤ Why do you think Heesoon did not want to write about her teaching?

➤ Why do you think Heesoon did not want to be observed by others while teaching?

➤ Discuss how you think you would react to each of these three modes of reflection.

➤ Hoover (1994) has noted that reflection is a learned activity. In what ways can teachers be prepared to talk effectively with a group of other teachers, to write about their teaching and to observe and be observed by other teachers?

From research to practice

I now present a framework that language teachers can consider if they want to engage in reflective language teaching. The framework attempts to bring together all of the topics discussed so far (although I also recognize that each chapter can be treated as a self-contained discussion of a specific aspect of reflective teaching). The framework has five core components as shown in Figure 14, and all five elements are interconnected in that one builds on the other and all need to be considered as a whole.

The five components are:

1. Provide different opportunities for reflection.
2. Build in ground rules.
3. Make provisions for time.
4. Provide for external input.
5. Develop trust.

Opportunities for reflection

The first and most important component of the framework involves providing opportunities for language teachers to reflect through a range of approaches that has been outlined and discussed in this book. These approaches include exploring one's beliefs and classroom practices, classroom communication patterns and interaction, critical incidents, language proficiency, and teachers' metaphors and maxims. These can be explored by the use of journal writing, classroom observations, group discussions, action research projects and concept mapping. Many of these approaches can be used alone by teachers or they can be used in combination with each other. For example, writing in teaching journals can assist teachers to focus on specific aspects of their development, and these can be used with or without classroom observations all of which can be used to document the teachers' beliefs and later compared with their theories-in-use. Use of a collaborative group of language teachers can create opportunities for sustained concentration and discussion in which mutual understandings can be constructed through talk. These groups can decide to collaborate in journal writing where they each keep journals, read each other's entries and later discuss the contents as a group. These discussions can also be recorded and later analysed for what issues occurred most frequently in discussions and the journals.

That said, individual teachers may have preferences for specific modes of reflection as was indicated in the case study discussed in this chapter. Heesoon showed a clear preference for talking with other colleagues in a group situation but did not really want to write about her teaching or have anyone observe her classes. The group was a forum for her to share her ideas and problems about her teaching life. The group atmosphere was light and a lot of humour was in evidence. Talking was sociable and enjoyable for Heesoon but writing was very stressful for her as was being observed, and as the conclusion to the case study suggested, we must decide what modes of reflection best suit our individual context and needs. Providing these opportunities for teachers to reflect is only the first component of this model of reflection. In order to establish an atmosphere where reflective practice in encouraged, several conditions must be met. These conditions include the following: negotiated ground rules, providing for different types of time, use of external input and providing for a low affective state.

Ground rules

Language teachers should now negotiate a set of built-in-rules or guidelines that teachers should follow in order to focus their reflections. For example, if teachers decided to reflect with a group of teachers, they must decide who will chair the group meetings. One answer might be a different chairperson for each meeting with a resulting level of responsibility (e.g. to provide a site and refreshments, and set the agenda and length of the meetings). For classroom observations, certain understandings need to be negotiated ahead of time and teachers should remember that reflection involves a three-part process of the event itself, recollection of the event, and review and response to the event (Richards and Lockhart, 1994). The case study reported in this chapter did not negotiate any specifics of the classroom observations ahead of time and this may have led to the teacher's eventual withdrawal from these observations. So, it is best to discuss specifics of each classroom observation ahead of time. For example, an actual teaching or learning episode can be a starting point for such classroom observations in order to stimulate reflection. Next the teaching event must be recollected in some way by the teacher and peer and/or group and preferably without judgement or evaluation. Events can be recollected through classroom observations and teaching journals. In addition, teachers who are observed by peers must also decide what the responsibility of the observer is, and if the class will be audiotaped, videotaped or not. The final stage involves the teacher who was observed returning to the event in order to examine its meaning for that teacher. Of course, all of the above activities and built-in guidelines cannot be accomplished quickly; like all valuable things, they take time. This introduces the next important component of the model: time.

Time

For practising teachers to be able to reflect on their work, time is a very important consideration and considered one of the main impediments to engaging in reflective teaching. I suggest teachers consider four different kinds of time and define each type before entering into the reflective process. These four are: *individual time, activity time, development time* and *period of reflection time*.

- *Individual time.* Practising teachers are very busy in their daily teaching and other related duties, and the amount of time any one teacher is willing to invest in his or her professional self-development will naturally vary. This can create a dilemma for the group if all the participants do not attend all the group meetings or participate fully in the activities; group cohesion may be harmed. Therefore, a certain level of commitment by individual participants in terms of time availability should be negotiated by the group at the start of the process.

- *Activity time.* Associated with the time each participant has to give to reflection is the time that should be considered when reflecting using specific activities. For example, for classroom observations, the number of times a class is to be observed should be negotiated ahead while also taking the first notion of time (individual) into consideration. The journal also needs time: time to write and time to read. In the case study reported on in this chapter this type of time was not negotiated ahead for the classroom observations or journal writing.

- *Development time.* Another aspect of time that is important for teachers to consider is the time it takes to develop both individually and as a group (if reflecting in a group). Simply put, some teachers need more time to develop than others and some teachers may not be ready (psychologically) to reflect because they have not reached that point in their life or career. In addition, other teachers may not want to reflect because they treat teaching as a job and not a profession. Perhaps Heesoon in the case study discussed in this chapter needed more time to develop especially when this reflection concerned looking closely at her classroom teaching and, as such, the observation process could have been delayed until she was ready. Analytical reflection, therefore, takes time and can only progress at a rate at which individual teachers are ready to reflect.

- *Period of reflection time.* The final aspect of time concerns the time frame for the reflective period as a whole that teachers are willing to commit to. Teachers (individually, pairs, groups) should consider how long they want to reflect? It is important to consider this for two reasons. When considering this aspect of time teachers should remember that critical reflection on one's teaching takes time, so the reflective period should be correspondingly long rather than short; otherwise, it might be time wasted. In addition, when teachers commit to having a fixed period in which to reflect, they also now know the exact period they can devote wholly to reflection. In the case study discussed in this chapter, the participants knew that it would last for one semester and so also knew when it would end.

External input

The previous three suggestions utilize the idea of probing and articulating personal theories, which is the core of teacher reflection. This process includes constructing and reconstructing real teaching experiences, and reflecting on personal beliefs about teaching. However, at this level, reflection only emphasizes personal experiences whether they are individual teachers or a group of teachers. There is also a need to compare the results of individual teachers and groups of teachers' reflective experiences to what others have discovered. Teachers need also to compare what they have learned from their reflections to what experts say in the form of theories learned from research and the literature on language teaching. So, there is also a need for inclusion of external input of some kind so the reflections can be further enriched with this input. This external input can come from professional journals, other teachers' observations and discussion especially if they have been written up in a teaching magazine, and also through journal and book publications. Individual teachers and a teacher development group can also attend conferences and seminars and report their findings to other teachers.

Trust

The first four components of the framework of reflective language teaching outlined above all pose some threat and associated anxiety for practising teachers when they engage in reflective teaching for any period of time. Therefore, a non-threatening environment should be encouraged by building up trust especially where peers and/or groups are observing each other and involved in group discussions. Ways of establishing trust can be incorporated into the reflective process itself, such as emphasizing description and observation over judgement in classroom observations and group discussions. It may also be an idea for peers and all group members to sign a paper that the results of the reflection cannot be disclosed without written permission from each member.

Professional development through reflective practice as it is outlined in this book is seen as entering a process of 'mental growth spurred from within' (Feiman-Namser and Floden, 1986: 523) in which teachers are supported in seeking their own direction of growth. Britten (1985) points out that the direction of this growth will depend on each teacher's needs, previous training, length of service of the teacher, career prospects and resources available. The experienced language teacher has already established a repertoire of teaching habits, and a relatively complex and integrated conceptual system for identifying classroom events. Consequently, any inservice programme should start with an exploration of where teachers are rather than a prescription for what the course leader thinks afflicts them so that they can prevent feelings of 'we've been here before' among the participants (Freeman, 1982). With such thoughts in mind I outline two workshops I conducted with second language teachers in Korea and Thailand, so that interested readers can explore the various topics these teachers generated for their reflections. Both workshops attempted to give ESL/EFL teachers an opportunity to find a focus to start their reflections on their own classroom practices and so that they could generate their own theories about teaching. The workshops were conducted in four phases and I explain each phase.

Phase I

This first phase of the workshop consisted of getting groups of five participants to sit in closed circles. Participants were given a blank index card when they walked into the room and asked *to reflect on a recent teaching practice or experience in the classroom, positive or negative, that caused them to stop and think about their teaching.* They were to write this on the blank card and then share it with the other members of the group. Each group was then asked *to rank the incidents in order of importance* and to write these on one blank card for each group. For the Korea TESOL group the important items were:

- using and teaching a grammar book;
- getting students out of the by 'rote' learning patterns and into a self-initiated, creative mindset;
- how do you help students think on their own?; students overcoming fear;
- is real communication activity possible in a beginners' group?;
- students' reading is parroting the text – are they understanding any of it and how can I tell?;
- tardy arrival of students;
- too many students in the classroom; student lack of attention – off-task behaviour;
- how to give feedback from mid-term exams;
- motivating the students;
- maintaining interest/attention with diverse groups;
- control of elementary school students.

The individual concerns at the Thai TESOL conference were:

- How can I get my students to study English? (from a Thai teacher).
- How can I get fresh ideas? (an American materials writer).

- How can we solve the entrance exam dilemma? (two teachers from Japan).
- How can I get teachers to be more confident? (a teacher educator in Hong Kong).
- What are 'qualified' teachers? (an American teacher in Korea).
- How can I get shy students from Asian countries to talk in class? (a teacher educator from the USA).

Phase I took about 10 minutes.

Phase II

For the second phase, the closed groups opened into one large group facing the blackboard. This second phase called for the participants to rank in order of importance five key dilemmas that they would like to discuss. I put a list of the five points pooled from each group on the blackboard as follows:

Group   A B C D E
Points
        1
        2
        3
        4
        5_____

Next, participants had to choose from the above list the five most problematic or interesting areas they would most like to discuss in detail.

The five areas that the Korea TESOL participants chose to talk about were:

- problems of class size
- student progress
- student motivation
- student fear of talking in English
- cultural dynamics

The five areas that the Thai group wanted to talk about were:

- entrance exams
- improving teacher's confidence
- students' lack of confidence

- cultural problems in teaching
- teachers making more informed decisions

Phase II took about 15 minutes.

Phase III

Next, five new sub-groups were set up under the five themes identified in phase II. Participants could choose to join any of these sub-groups to discuss specific problems. A summary of the topics each group talked about were presented in the form of guidelines in phase IV, the final phase. It worked out that the participants were, more or less, evenly numbered in each sub-group with no one theme attracting more participants than another.

Phase III took about 20 minutes.

Phase IV

Finally, each sub-group reported back to the main group in order to share their reflection on that theme. For example, the groups at the *Korea TESOL chose five group topics and came up with some guidelines for teachers:*

- Group 1: Large classes. Definition: 50–70 students of different ages; guideline: do group/pair work whenever possible.
- Group 2: Student progress; guideline: teachers should have sound methods of assessment and give feedback.
- Group 3: Motivation; guideline: topics must have relevance to students' lives and experiences.
- Group 4: Student fear of talking; guideline: prepare students with exposure to language that will appear in the activity.
- Group 5: Cultural dynamics; guideline: avoid confrontation.

Examples from the groups at the Thai TESOL included:

- Group 1: Entrance exams; guideline: listening and speaking component should be added in the national tests of Japan, Korea and Thailand.
- Group 2: Improving teacher's confidence; guideline: opportunities for professional upgrading.

Phase IV took about 10 minutes.

For language teachers wishing to conduct a similar workshop in different contexts, it is important to remember that the participants must be advised to take an active role in all the activities. Also, 60 minutes should be enough time to complete the workshop. What was absent from the above workshops in Thailand and Korea was follow-up. Language teachers need to continue their focused reflections on the topics generated in the workshop with other groups of teachers by using the methods and activities presented in this book. Groups of teachers can then compare what they have discovered and thus contribute to the professional development of all concerned.

It is evident from the diverse topics in each workshop that EFL teachers have a lot to say; the only problem is that they often do not have a forum in which they can present their ideas. The type of talking and sharing in the workshops frees ESL teachers from impulsive and routine behaviour. Furthermore, this type of reflection allows the teacher to act in a deliberative, intentional manner and to avoid the feeling that theory is not applicable to their teaching lives. A group of teachers who meet and talk about teaching (as happened in the workshop outlined in this chapter) can draw on their own experiences and become more confident that what they may be doing in the classroom is theoretically and practically sound. In addition, teacher educators can use the same system to become proactive thinkers about strategies that may help them in their classrooms.

Reflection

➢ Copeland, *et al.* (1993: 348) maintain that 'The demonstration of reflective practice is seen to exist along a continuum; people vary in opportunity, ability, or propensity to reflect. Therefore, they say it may be unreasonable to expect teachers consistently to engage in reflection at every moment'. What is your opinion of this statement?

➢ Some teachers suggest some barriers which may be problematic for successful achievement of reflective practice such as teachers need time and opportunity for development and exposing oneself and one's opinions in a group of strangers can lead to vulnerability. How would you address these problems?

➢ Which areas of your teaching do you think you need to develop?

➢ Start the process of self-monitoring your teaching and try to put in place as many of the reflections *on* (classroom communication, metaphors and maxims, beliefs and practices, etc.) and *with* (teaching journals, classroom observations, action research, etc.) opportunities as presented in this book.

➤ Try to collaborate with a critical friend and put in place as many of the reflections *on* (classroom communication, metaphors and maxims, beliefs and practices, etc.) and *with* (teaching journals, classroom observations, action research, etc.) opportunities as presented in this book.

➤ Try to form a teacher development group and try to put in place as many of the reflections *on* (classroom communication, metaphors and maxims, beliefs and practices, etc.) and *with* (teaching journals, classroom observations, action research, etc.) opportunities as presented in this book.

Conclusion

One question I think important to ask now is: 'How would you recognize a reflective language teacher if you saw one?'. I see a reflective second language teacher as one who takes responsibility for his or her own knowledge construction by engaging in reflective activities. These activities can include any or all of the following: conducting an action research project, keeping a teaching journal, video and/or audiotaping a class or classes and observing peers teaching, talking with a group of teachers, developing a teacher portfolio and/or utilizing other methods and activities that have been covered in this book. A common benefit derived from all these methods is that they can provide second language teachers with support and different means for reflecting on their teaching. This form of professional development goes beyond one-day 'dog-and-pony shows' that feature a motivational speaker and often rely on 'quick-fix' scenarios or teachers are provided with 'teacher-proof' activities to replicate in the classroom in order to improve their practice. As Kumaravadivelu (2003: 17) has suggested, second language teachers should enter into 'a continual process of self-reflection and self-renewal' so that they can 'construct their own personal theory of teaching'.

Chapter scenario

A group of EFL teachers in Russia, Gallina, Gregor and Nadia, were concerned that their students were not speaking enough English during their classes and worse still, some consistently spoke Russian during their classes. So, they decided to write teaching journals and meet as a group once a week for a few weeks to discuss this problem. After a few weeks talking about this problem during the group meetings one of the group members, Gallina, reflected on this problem of 'getting them to talk more in class' and wrote in her journal as follows: 'I am unsatisfied; I had wanted them to talk more. I was not happy with [a student], speaking a lot of Russian yesterday and so I scolded him in front of the class.' Gallina then revealed to the group that she was now becoming even more concerned with the situation in her class because her students have gone silent nearly totally and do not even speak in Russian. So Gallina, together with the other group members further discussed her dilemma of trying to get her students to speak more English in her conversation classes over the following three weeks. As Gregor and Nadia had a similar but less severe problem in some of their classes they all (as a group) decided to make a general plan to observer each other's class for a period of four weeks. The first thing they suggested was that Gallina and the other teachers should not fill in any silence in their classes and to let the students fill in any gaps in silence in English themselves. Also, they suggested that they could scaffold more during the class by providing starter answers to questions in English and to introduce more structured topics during the class so that the students would not feel intimated when speaking English. Over time, they all incorporated these suggestions into their classes and as a result, their students began to speak more English during the classes.

Reflection

- What do you think of the procedures the group adopted to facilitate their reflections?
- If you were a member of a teacher development group that decided to focus their discussion topic on getting students to speak more (English) in class, what procedures would you suggest the group adopt to investigate this?
- Outline a detailed plan (including a timeline) for this group to investigate the topic for critical reflection.

References

Acheson, K. A. and Gall, M. D. (1987). *Techniques in the Clinical Supervision of Teachers*. New York: Longman.

Antonacci, P. A. (1991). Students search for meaning in the text through semantic mapping. *Social Education*, 55, 174–5, 194.

Bachman, L. F. (1990). *Fundamental Consideration in Language Testing*. Oxford: Oxford University Press.

Baciu, S. (1998). Language awareness workshops: A teacher training program component in project PROSPER. In J. C. Richards (ed.), *Teaching in Action*, (pp. 23–9). Alexandria, VA: TESOL.

Bailey, K. M. (1990). The use of diary studies in teacher education programs. In J. C. Richards and D. Nunan (eds), *Second Language Teacher Education*, (pp. 215–26). New York, Cambridge University Press.

————. (2001). Action research, teacher research, and classroom research in language teaching. In M. Celce-Murcia (ed), *Teaching English as a Second or Foreign Language* (3rd edn) (pp. 489–98). Boston: Heinle and Heinle.

Barnes, D. (1976). *From Communication to curriculum*. Middlesex: Penguin.

Bartlett, L. (1990). Teacher development through reflective teaching. In J. C. Richards, and D. Nunan (eds), *Second Language Teacher Education* (pp. 202–14). New York: Cambridge University Press.

Belbin, R. M. (1993). *Team Roles at Work*. Oxford: Butterfield-Heinemann.

Bell, J. S. (2002). Narrative inquiry: more than just telling stories. *TESOL Quarterly*, 36 207–13.

Belleck, A. Kiebard, H. Hyman, R. and Smith, F. (1966). *The Language of the Classroom*. New York: Teachers College Press.

Bergsgaard, M. and Ellis, M. (2002). Inward: The journey toward authenticity through self-observing. *Journal of Educational Thought*, 36, 53–68.

Berliner, D. (1990). If the metaphor fits why not wear it? The teacher as executive. *Theory into Practice*, 29, 85–93.

Berry, R. (1990). The role of language improvement in in-service teacher training: killing two birds with one stone. *System*, 18, 97–105.

Block, D. (1992). Metaphors we teach and learn by. *Prospect*, 7, 42–55.

Borg, S. (1998). Teachers' pedagogical systems and grammar teaching: a qualitative study. *TESOL Quarterly*, 32, 9–38.

———— (2003). Teacher cognition in language teaching: A review of research on what language teachers think, know, believe, and do. *Language Teaching*, 36, 81–109.

Breen, M. P. (1991). Understanding the language teacher. In R. Phillipson, E. Kellerman, L. Selinker, M. Sharwood Smith and M. Swain (eds), *Foreign/Second Language Pedagogy Research* (pp. 213–33). Clevedon, UK: Multilingual Matters.

Breen, M. P., Hird, B., Milton, M., Oliver, R. and Thwaite, A. (2001). Making sense of language teaching: teachers' principles and classroom practices. *Applied Linguistics*, 22, 470–501.

Britten, D. (1985). Teacher training in ELT: Part 1. *Language Teaching*, 18, 112–28.

Brock, M., Yu, B. and Wong, M. (1992). 'Journalling' together: Collaborative diary-keeping and teacher development. In J. Flowerdew, M. Brock, and S. Hsia (eds) *Perspectives on Second Language Teacher Development*. (pp. 295–307). Hong Kong: City University of Hong Kong.

Brookfield, S. D. (1990). *The Skilful Teacher*. San Francisco: Jossey Bass.

Brown, J. D. and Wolfe-Quintero, K. (1997). Teacher portfolios for evaluation: A great idea? Or a waste of time? *The Language Teacher*, 28–30.

Bullough, R. V. (1997). Practicing theory and theorizing practice in teacher education. In J. Loughran and T. Russell (eds), *Teaching About Teaching: Purpose, Passion and Pedagogy in Teacher Education* (pp. 13–31). London: Falmer Press.

Burns, A. (1992). Teacher beliefs and their influence on classroom practice. *Prospect*, 7, 65.

————(1995). Teacher-researchers: Perspectives on teacher action research and curriculum renewal. In A. Burns and S. Hood (eds), *Teachers' Voices: Exploring Course Design in a Changing Curriculum* (pp. 3–29). Sydney: NCELTR, Macquarie University.

———— (1999). *Collaborative Action Research for English Language Teachers*. Cambridge: Cambridge University Press.

Burton, J. (2005). The importance of teachers writing on TESOL. *TESL-EJ*, 9.

Cazden, C. (1988). *Classroom discourse: the language of teaching and learning*. Portsmouth, NH. Heinemann.

Clair, N. (1998). Teacher study groups: persistent questions in a promising approach. *TESOL Quarterly*, 32, 465–92.

Clandinin, D. J. (1986) *Classroom Practice: Teacher Images in Action*. London: Falmer Press.

Clarke, A. (1995). Professional development in practicum settings: reflective practice under scrutiny. *Teaching and Teacher Education*, 11, 243–61.

Copeland, W. D., Birmingham, C., DeLaCruz, E. and Lewin B. (1993). The reflective practitioner in teaching: toward a research agenda. *Teaching and Teacher Education*, 9, 347–59.

Cruickshank, D. and Applegate, J. (1981). Reflective teaching as a strategy for teacher growth. *Educational Leadership*, 38, 553–4.

Curtis, A. (2001). Hong Kong secondary school teachers' first experiences of action research. *PAC Journal* ,1, 65–78.

Day, C. (1993). Reflection: a necessary but not sufficient condition for teacher development. *British Educational Research Journal*, 19, 83–93.

————(1998). Working with the different selves of teachers: Beyond comfortable collaboration. *Education Action Research 6*, 255–275.

Day, R. (1990). Teacher observation in second language teacher education. In J. C. Richards. and D. Nunan (eds), *Second Language Teacher Education* (pp.43–61). Cambridge: Cambridge University Press.

Dewey, J. (1933). *How We Think*. Madison, WI: University of Wisconsin Press.

Dickmeyer, N. (1989). Metaphor, model, and theory in education research. *Teachers College Record*, 91, 151–60.

Fanselow, J. F. (1987). *Breaking Rules: Generating and Exploring Alternatives in Language Teaching*. White Plains, NY: Longman.

————(1988). 'Let's see': contrasting conversations about teaching. *TESOL Quarterly* 22, 113–30.

————(1992). *Contrasting Conversations*. White Plains, NY: Longman.

Farrell, T. S. C. (1996). 'The Look': Some observations on observation. *The Teacher Trainer*, 21, 11.

————(1998a). EFL teacher development through journal writing. *RELC Journal*, 29, 92–109.

————(1998b). Unraveling reflective teaching. *TESOL Reporter*, 32, 1–10

————(1998c). Critical friendship in ELT. *Prospect: The Australian TESOL Journal*, 13, 78–88.

————(1998d). Principles and practices of reflective teaching. *English Teaching Forum*, 36 (Oct–Dec): 10–17.

————(1998e). Communicating with colleagues of a different Culture. In J. C. Richards (ed.). *Teaching in Action: Case Studies from Second Language Classrooms* (pp. 125–8). Alexandria, Virginia: TESOL Publications.

————(1999a). Reflective practice in a teacher development group. *System*, 27, 157–72.

————(1999b). Reflective teaching: a case study. *Asian Journal of English Teaching*, 9, 105–14.

————(1999c). Teachers talking about teaching: Creating Conditions for reflection. *TESL-EJ*, 4, 1–16.

————(1999d). The reflective assignment: unlocking pre-service English teachers' beliefs on grammar teaching. *RELC Journal*, 30, 1–17.

————(2001a). Tailoring reflection to individual needs: a TESOL case study. *International Journal of Education for Teaching*, 21, 23–38.

————(2001b). Critical friendships: colleagues helping each other develop. *ELT Journal*, 52, 368–74.

————(2002). Reflecting on teacher professional development with teaching portfolios. *Guidelines*, 24, 4–8.

————(2003). 'Should I give the rule or get on with the lesson?' The case for case studies in grammar teacher education. In D. Liu. and P. Masters (eds). *Grammar Case Studies in Teacher Education* (pp. 125–35). Alexandria, VA: TESOL USA.

————(2004a). *Reflective Practice in Action*. Thousand Oaks, CA: Corwin Press.

————(2004b). *Reflecting on Classroom Communication in Asia*. Singapore: Longman.

————(2004c). The tree of life: from language teacher to language teacher educator. In D. Hayes (ed.), *Trainer Development: Principles and Practices* (pp. 51–62). Melbourne: Language Awareness

————(2006a). Learning to teach English language: imposing order. *System*, 34, 211–21.

————(2006b). 'The teacher is an octopus': uncovering preservice English language teachers' prior beliefs through metaphor analysis. *RELC Journal*, 37, 239–51.

————(2006c). Reflective practice in action: a case study of a writing teacher's reflections on practice. *TESL Canada Journal*, 23, 77–90.

Farrell, T. S. C. (ed.) (2006d). *Language Teacher Research in Asia*. Alexandria, VA: TESOL Publications.

Farrell, T. S. C. (2006e). *Succeeding with English Language Learners: A Guide for Beginning Teachers*. Thousand Oaks, CA: Corwin Press.

————(2007a). Failing the practicum: narrowing the gap between expectation and reality with reflective practice. *TESOL Quarterly*, 41(1), 193–201.

————(2007b). Promoting reflective practice in language teacher education with microteaching. *Asian Journal of English Language Teaching* (AJELT), 17.

————(2008/forthcoming). Critical incidents in ELT initial teacher training. *ELT Journal*.

Farrell, T. S. C. and Lee, F. T. (2003). Bridging the gap between words and action. In Hadley, G. (ed.) *Asian Voices: Action Research in Action* (pp. 9–15). Singapore: SEAMEO Regional Language Centre.

Farrell, T. S. C. and Lim. P. (2005). Grammar teaching: a case study of teachers' beliefs and classroom practices *TESL-EJ* (September 2005).

Feiman-Nemser, S. and Floden, R. (1986). The cultures of teaching. In M. C. Wittrock (ed.), *Handbook of Research on Teaching* (pp. 505–25). New York: Macmillan.

Fischer, F. Bruhn, J., Grasel, C. and Mandl, H. (2002). Fostering collaborative knowledge construction with visualization tools. *Learning and Instruction*, 12, 213–32.

Freeman, D. (1989). Teacher training, development, and decision-making. *TESOL Quarterly*, 23, 17–47.

————(1996). Redefining the relationship between research and what teachers know. In K. M. Bailey, and. Nunan (eds.), *Voices from the Language Classroom: Qualitative Research in Second Language Education* (pp. 88–115). Cambridge: Cambridge University Press.

Freeman, D. and Richards, J. C. (1993). Conceptions of teaching and the education of second language teachers. *TESOL Quarterly*, 27, 193–216.

Freeman, D. and Johnson, K. (1998). Reconceptualizing the knowledge-base of language teacher education. *TESOL Quarterly*, 32, 397–417.

Gaies, S. (1991). ELT in the 1990s. *JALT Journal*, 13, 7–21.

Gebhard, J. G. (1999). Reflecting through a teaching journal. In J. G. Gebhard and R. Oprandy (eds.), *Language Teaching Awareness* (pp. 78–98). New York: Cambridge University Press.

Golby, M. and Appleby, R. (1995). Reflective practice through critical friendship: some possibilities. *Cambridge Journal of Education* 25, 149–60.

Gootesman, B. (2000). *Peer Coaching for Educators* (2nd edn). London: The Scarecrow Press.

Gow,. L. Kember, D. and McKay, J. (1996). Improving student learning through action research into teaching. In D. Watkins and J. B. Biggs (eds), *The Chinese Learner: Cultural, Psychological and Contextual Influences* (pp. 243–65). Hong Kong: CERC and ACER.

Hatton, N. and Smith, D. (1995). Reflection in teacher education: towards definition and implementation. *Teaching and Teacher Education*, 11, 33–39.

Head, K. and Taylor, P. (1997). *Readings in Teacher Development*. London: Heinemann.

Heaton. J. B. (1981). *Using English in the Classroom*. Singapore: Longman.

Ho, B. and Richards, J. C. (1993). Reflective thinking through teacher journal writing: myths and realities *Prospect*, 8, 7–24.

Hoover, L. (1994). Reflective writing as a window on pre-service teachers' thought processes. *Teacher and Teacher Education*, 10, 83–93.

Jay, J. K. and Johnson, K. L. (2002). Capturing complexity: a typology of reflective practice for teacher education. *Teaching and Teacher Education*, 18, 73–85.

Jarvis, J. (1996). Using diaries for teacher refection on in-service courses. In T. Hedge and N. Whitney (eds), *Power, Pedagogy and Practice*, (pp. 307–23). Oxford: Oxford University Press.

Johnson, K. E. (1994). The emerging beliefs and instructional practices of preservice English as a second language teachers. *Teaching and Teacher Education*, 10, 439–52.

————(1995). *Understanding Communication in Second Language Classrooms*. New York: Cambridge University Press.

————(1999). *Understanding Language Teaching*: *Reasoning in Action*. Boston: Heinle and Heinle.

Johnson, K. E. and Glombek, P. (2002). *Teacher's Narrative Inquiry As Professional Development*. New York: Cambridge University Press.

Johnson. R. K. (1990). Developing teachers' language resources. In J. C. Richards and D. Nunan (eds), *Second Language Teacher Education*, (pp. 269–81). New York: Cambridge University Press.

Kagan, D. M. (1992). Professional growth among pre-service and beginning teachers. *Review of Educational Research*, 64, 129–69.

Kaufman. D. and Brooks, G., J. (1996). Interdisciplinary collaboration in teacher education: a constructivist approach. *TESOL Quarterly*, 30, 231–51.

Keiko, S. and Gaies, S. J. (2002). Beliefs and professional identity. *Language Teacher*, 26, 7–11.

Killon, J. and Todnew, G. (1991). A process of personal theory building. *Educational Leadership*, 48, 14–16.

Kirk, W. and Walter, G. (1981). Teacher support groups serve to minimize teacher burnout: principles for organizing. *Education*, 102, 147–50.

Knezedivc, B. (2001). Action research. *IATEFL Teacher Development SIG Newsletter*, 1, 10–12.

Krashen, S. (1981). *Second Language Acquisition and Second Language Learning*. Oxford: Pergamon.

————(1982). *Principles and Practices in Second Language Acquisition*. Oxford: Pergamon.

Kumaravadivelu, B. (2003). *Beyond Methods: Macrostrategies for Language Teaching*. New Haven, CT: Yale University Press.

Lakeoff, G. and Johnson, M (1980) *Metaphors We Live by*. Chicago: University of Chicago Press.

Lange, D. (1990). A blueprint for a teacher development program. In J. C. Richards and D. Nunan (eds), *Second Language Teacher Education* (pp. 245–68). New York: Cambridge University Press.

Lafayette, R. (1993). Subject matter content: what every foreign language teacher needs to know. In G. Guntermann, (ed.), *Developing Language Teachers for a Changing World*, (pp. 124–58). Illinois: National Textbook Company.

Little. J. W. (1993). Teachers professional development in a climate of educational reform. *Educational Evaluation and Policy Analysis* 15, 129–51.

Long, M. H. and Crookes, G. (1986). *Intervention Points in Second Language Classroom Processes*. Paper presented at the RELC Conference, Singapore 21–25 Aril, 1986.

Long, M. H. and Sato, C. (1983). Classroom foreigner talk discourse: forms and functions of teachers' questions. In H. Seliger and M. Long (eds), *Classroom Oriented Research in Second Language Acquisition*, Rowley, MA: Newbury House.

Lortie, D. C. (1975). *Schoolteacher: A Sociological Study*. Chicago: University of Chicago Press.

McCabe, A. (2002). Narratives: a wellspring for development. In J. Edge (ed.), *Continuing Professional Development* (pp. 82–89). UK: IATEFL

McDonough, J. (1994). A teacher looks at teachers' diaries, *English Language Teaching Journal*, 18, 57–65.

Maley, A. (1986). Xanadu—'A miracle of rare device': the teaching of English in China. In J. M. Valdes (ed.), *Culture Bound* (pp. 102–11). Cambridge: Cambridge University Press.

Mann, S. (2005). The language teacher's development. *Language Teaching*, 38, 103–18.

Matlin, M. and Short, K. G., (1991). How our teacher study group sparks change. *Educational Leadership*, 49, 68.

Measor, L. (1985). Critical incidents in the classroom: identities, choices and careers. In S. J. Ball and I. V. Goodson (eds). *Teachers' Lives and Careers* (pp. 61–77). London: Falmer Press.

Medgyes, P. (2001). When the teacher is a non-native speaker. In M. Celce-Murcia (ed.), *Teaching English as a Second or Foreign Language* (3rd edn) (pp. 415–27). Boston: Heinle and Heinle.

Meijer, P. C. Verloop, N. and Beijaard, D. (1999). Exploring language teachers' practical knowledge about teaching reading comprehension. *Teaching and Teacher Education*, 15, 59–84.

Mergendoller, R. and Sacks, C. (1994). Concerning the relationship between teachers' theoretical orientations toward reading and their concept maps. *Teaching and Teacher Education*, 10, 589–99.

Merryfield, M. (1993). Reflective practice in global education: Strategies for teacher educators. *Theory Into Practice*, 32, 27–32.

McMeninman, M., Cumming, J., Wilson, J., Stevenson, P. and Sim, C. (2003). *Teacher Knowledge in Action*. Department of Education, Training and Youth Affairs, Australia.

Moon, J. and Boullon, R. (1997). Reluctance to reflect: issues in professional development In D. Hayes (ed.), *In-service Teacher Development: International Perspectives*. London: Prentice Hall

Munby, H. and Russell, T. (1989). Educating the reflective teacher: An essay review. *Journal of Curriculum Studies*, 2, 71–80.

Novak, J. D. (1990). Concept maps and Vee diagrams: two metacognitive tools to facilitate meaningful learning. *Instructional Science*, 19, 1–25.

Novak J. D and Gowin D. B. (1984). *Learning How to Learn*. New York: Cambridge University Press.

Oberg, A. and Blades, C. (1990). The spoken and the unspoken: the story of an educator. *Phenomonology + Pedagogy*, 8, 161–80.

Oprandy, R. Golden, L and Shiomi, K. (1999). Teachers talking about teaching. In J. Gebhard and R. Oprandy (eds), *Language Teaching Awareness* (pp. 149–71). New York: Cambridge University Press.

Oliphant, K. (2003). Teacher development groups: growth through cooperation. In G. Crookes. *A Practicum in TESOL*. (pp. 203–14). New York: Cambridge University Press.

Olshtain, E. and Kupferberg, I. (1998). Relective-narrative discourse of FL teachers exhibits professional knowledge. *Language Teaching Research*, 2, 185–202.

Oxford, R. L., Tomlinson, S., Barcelos, A., Harrington, C., Lavine, R. Z., Saleh, A. and Longhini, A. (1998). Clashing metaphors about classroom teachers: toward a systematic typology for the language teaching field. *System*, 26, 3–50.

Pajak, E. F. (1986) Psychoanalysis, teaching, and supervision. *Journal of Curriculum and Supervision*, 1, 122–31.

Pajares , M. F., (1992). Teachers' beliefs and educational research: cleaning up a messy construct. *Review of Educational Research*, 62, 307–32.

Palmer, P. J. (1998). *The Courage to Teach*. San Francisco, CA: Jossey-Bass.

Pennington, M. C. (1992). Reflecting on teaching and learning: a developmental focus for the second language classroom. In J. Flowerdew, M. Brock and S. Hsia (eds), *Perspectives on Second Language Teacher Education* (pp. 47–65). Kowloon: City Polytechnic of Hong Kong.

————(1995). The teacher change cycle. *TESOL Quarterly*, 29, 705–31.

Pennington, M. C. Costa, V. So, S., Shing, J. Hirose, K. and Niedzielski, K. (1997). The teaching of English-as-a-second-language writing in the Asia-Pacific Region: a cross-country comparison. *RELC Journal*, 28, 120–43.

Philips, S. (1983). *The Invisible Culture: Communication in Classroom and Community on the Warm Springs Indian Reservation*. Prospect Heights, Illinois: Waveland Press

Pica, T., Young, R. and Doughty, C. (1987). The impact of interaction on comprehension. *TESOL Quarterly*, 21, 737–58.

Pica, T. and Long, M. H. (1986). The classroom linguistic and conversational performance of experienced and inexperienced teachers. In Day, R. (ed), *Talking to learn: Conversation in Second Language Acquisition*, Rowley, MA: Newbury House.

Provenzo, E. F., McCloskey, G. N., Kottamp, R. B. and Cohn, M. M. (1989). Metaphor and the meaning of language of teachers. *Teachers College Record*, 90, 551–73.

Richards, J. c. (1990). Beyond training: Approaches to teacher education in language teaching. *Language Teacher*, 14, 3–8.

————(1996). Teachers' maxims in language teaching. *TESOL Quarterly*, 30, 281–96.

————(1998). *Beyond Training*. New York: Cambridge University Press.

Richards, J. C. (ed.), (1998). *Teaching in Action: Case Studies From Second Language Classrooms*. Alexandria, VA: TESOL.

Richards, J. C. and Farrell, T. S. C (2005). *Professional Development for Language Teachers*. New York: Cambridge University Press.

Richards, J. C. Gallo, P. B. and Renandya, W. A. (2001). Exploring teachers' beliefs and the processes of Change. *PAC Journal*, 1, 41–58

Richards, J. C. and Lockhard, C. (1994). *Reflective Teaching*. New York: Cambridge University Press.

Richards, J. C. and Nunan, D. (eds), (1990). *Second Language Teacher Education*. New York: Cambridge University Press.

Richards, J. C. Ho, B. and Giblin, K. (1996). Learning how to teaching in the RSA Cert. In D. Freeman and J. C. Richards (eds), *Teacher Learning in Language Teaching*, (pp. 242–59). New York: Cambridge University Press.

Richard-Amato P., A. (1988). *Making It Happen*. New York: Longman.

Richardson, L. (1997). *Fields of Play: Constructing an Academic Life*. New Brunswick, NJ: Rutgers University Press.

Richert, A. (1990). Teaching teachers to reflect: a consideration of program structure. *Journal of Curriculum Studies*, 22, 509–27.

Rivers W. (1981). *Teaching Foreign Language Skills* (2nd edn). Chicago: University of Chicago Press.

Roberts, J. (1998). *Language Teacher Education*. London: Arnold.

Robbins, P. (1991). *How to Plan and Implement a Peer Coaching Programme*. Alexandra, VA: ASCD.

Sagor, R. (1992). How to Conduct Collaborative Action Research. Alexandria, Virginia: Association for Supervision and Curriculum Development.

Sagliano, J. Sagliano, M. and Stewart, T. (1998). Peer coaching through team teaching: three cases of *teacher development. Asia-Pacific Journal of Teacher Education and Development*, 1, 73–82.

Schön, D. A. (1983). *The Reflective Practitioner: How Professionals Think in Action*. New York: Basic Books.

————(1987). *Educating the Reflective Practitioner: Towards a New Design for Teaching and Learning in the Profession*. San Francisco: Jossey-Bass.

Schrange, M. (1990). *Shared Minds*. New York: Random House.

Seaman, A., Sweeney, B., Meadows, P. and Sweeney, M. (1997) Collaboration, reflection, and professional growth: a mentoring programme for adult ESL teachers, *TESOL Journal*, 7, 31–4.

Senge, P. M. (1990). *The Fifth Discipline*. New York: Bantam Books.

Senior, R (2006). *The Experience of Language Teaching*. New York: Cambridge University Press.

Shi, L. and Cumming, A. (1995). Teachers' conceptions of second-language writing instruction: five case studies. *Journal of Second Language Writing*, 4, 87–111.

Shin, S. J. (2003). The reflective L2 writing teacher. *ELT Journal*, 57, 3–11.

Shulman, J. (ed), (1992). *Case Methods in Teacher Education*. New York: Teachers College Press.

Siemens, G. (2004). *Connectivism: A Learning Theory for the Digital Age* http://www.elearnspace.org/Articles/connectivism.htm (Retrieved 17 January, 2007).

Sitamparam, S. and Dhamotharan, M. (1992). Peer networking: towards self-direction in teacher development. *English Teaching Forum*, 12–15.

Stanley, C. (1998). A framework for teacher reflectivity. *TESOL Quarterly*, 32, 584–91.

Stenhouse, L. (1975). *An Introduction to Curriculum Research and Development*. London: Heinemann.

Stewart, T. (2001). The value of action research in exploring methodology: a case of instruction on questioning in debate. *PAC Journal*, 1, 79–92.

Stewart, T., Sagliano, M., and Sagliano, J. (2002). Merging expertise: promoting partnerships between language and content specialists. In J. Crandall and D. Kaufman (eds), *Content-based Language Instruction*. Alexandria, VA: TESOL, Inc.

Struman, P. (1992). Team teaching: a case study from Japan. In D. Nunan (ed.), *Collaborative Language Learning and Teaching* (pp. 141–61). Cambridge: Cambridge University Press.

Swain, M. (1999). Integrating language and content teaching through collaborative tasks. In C. Ward and W. Renandya (eds), *Language Teaching: New Insights for the Language Teacher*. Singapore: RELC.

Taggart, G. and Wilson, A. P. (1998). *Promoting Reflective Thinking in Teachers*. Thousand Oaks, CA: Corwin Press.

Tedick, D. (ed), (2005). Second language teacher education: International Perspectives. Mahwah, NJ: Lawrence Erlbaum Associates.

Thiel, T. (1999). Reflections on critical incidents. *Prospect*, 14, 44–52.

Towndrow, P. (2004). Reflections of an on-line tutor. *ELT Journal*, 58, 174–82.

Tripp, D. (1993). *Critical Incidents in Teaching*. London: Routledge.

Tsui, A. (1995). *Introducing Classroom Interaction*. London: Penguin.

————(2003). *Understanding Expertise in Teaching: Case Studies of ESL Teachers*. New York: Cambridge University Press.

Ur, P. (1996). *A Course in Language Teaching: Practice and Theory*. Cambridge: Cambridge University Press.

Van Bruggen, J. M., Kirschner, P. A. and Jochems, W. (2002). External representation of argumentation in CSCL and the management of cognitive load. *Learning and Instruction*, 12, 121–38.

Van Manen V. M. (1977). Linking ways of knowing with ways of being practical. *Curriculum Inquiry*, 6, 205–28.

Wajnryb, R. (1992). *Classroom Observation Tasks*. Cambridge: Cambridge University Press.

Wallace, M. J. (1991). *Teacher Training: A Reflective Approach*. Cambridge: Cambridge University Press.

————(1996). Structured reflection: the role of the professional project in training ESL teachers. In D. Freeman and J. C. Richards (eds), *Teacher Learning in Language Teaching* (pp. 281–94). New York: Cambridge University Press.

————(1998). *Action Research for Language Teachers*. Cambridge: Cambridge University Press.

Wallace, M. J. and Woolger, D. (1991). Improving the ELT supervisory dialogue: the Sri Lanka experience. *ELT Journal*, 45, 320–27.

Wassermann, S. (1993). *Getting Down to Cases: Learning to Teach with Case Studies*. New York: Teachers College.

Watson-Gegeo, K. A. (1988). Ethnography in ESL: defining the essentials. *TESOL Quarterly*, 22, 575–92.

Williams, M. (1989). A developmental view of classroom observation. *ELT Journal*, 43, 85–91.

Williams, M. and Burden, R. (1997). *Psychology for Language Teachers: A Social Constructivist Approach*. Cambridge: Cambridge University Press.

Willis, J. (1981). *Teaching English Through English*. London: Longman.

Wilson, V. A. (1998). Concept maps can increase understanding for students and teachers. *The Teaching Professor*, 8, August, September.

Woods, D. (1996). *Teacher Cognition in Language Teaching*. Cambridge: Cambridge University Press.

Zaid, M. A. (1995). Semantic mapping in communicative language teaching. *English Teaching Forum*, 33, 6–11.

Zeichner, K. and Liston, O. (1996). *Reflective Teaching*. New Jersey: Lawrence Earlbaum.

Index